It's Another Ace Book from CGP

This book is for 12-14 year olds.

It's packed with all the <u>really important stuff</u>
you need to know about <u>Henry V</u> if you want to do well
in your Key Stage Three SAT Paper 2.

We've stuck loads of pictures and jokes in to make it more fun
— so you'll <u>actually use it</u>.

Simple as that.

CGP are just the best

The central aim of Coordination Group Publications is to produce
top quality books that are carefully written, immaculately
presented and marvellously funny — whilst always making sure
they exactly cover the National Curriculum for each subject.

And then we supply them to as many people as we possibly
can, as <u>cheaply</u> as we possibly can.

Buy our books — they're ace

Contents

Published by Coordination Group Publications Ltd.

Contributors:
Simon Cook   BA Hons.
Taissa Csáky   BA Hons.
Gemma Hallam   MA Hons. (Cantab)
Iain Nash   BSc.
and
William Shakespeare

ISBN   1-84146-140-7

Groovy website: www.cgpbooks.co.uk

Jolly bits of clipart from CorelDRAW

Printed by Elanders Hindson, Newcastle upon Tyne.

0600

Three Key Things To Remember

You've got to write about *Henry V* for your SAT — whether you like it or not.
It <u>doesn't matter</u> if you think it's <u>naff</u> or <u>boring</u> — just remember, it's <u>not</u> impossible.

What it's *All About*

Henry V is jam-packed full of <u>story</u>. There's a <u>war</u> between England and France, loads of politics, a few <u>funny scenes</u> and a <u>marriage</u> at the end of it all. <u>King Henry V</u> of England is the <u>hero</u> (not surprisingly), but there are <u>loads</u> of other characters too.

There are *Lots* of *Characters* to *Look Out for*

This <u>isn't</u> just a play about <u>Kings</u>, <u>Dukes</u> and <u>Knights</u>. It's about the <u>whole</u> of society — <u>ordinary soldiers</u>, <u>Welshmen</u>, <u>Irishmen</u>, <u>Scotsmen</u>, even <u>thieves</u> and <u>drunks</u>.

It's also about <u>uniting</u> against your <u>enemies</u>. Even though the English army is made up of all these different people, they come together to <u>defeat</u> a much bigger French army in the play.

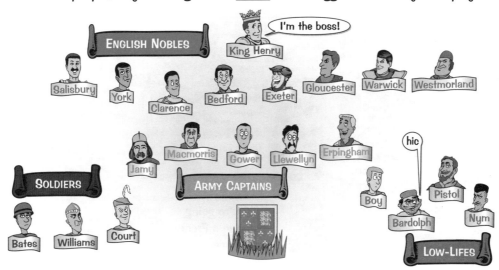

One of the key things to look out for is the <u>attitudes</u> of <u>King Henry</u> and the <u>nobles</u>, compared with the <u>attitudes</u> of the <u>ordinary soldiers</u>. They've all got <u>different opinions</u> on the war and on <u>who's responsible</u> for it — the <u>King</u> himself or someone else.

Uh oh — *it's Written in* *Really Old English*

(1) The play's written in the <u>sort of English</u> people spoke <u>at the time</u> it was written. Shakespeare was a writer and poet who lived between <u>1564</u> and <u>1616</u>. He wrote *Henry V* around <u>1599</u>. English has really <u>changed</u> since then.

(2) A lot of the play is written in <u>poetry</u> — that makes the speeches <u>tricky</u> to understand. The characters use lots of <u>weird words</u>, and their <u>sentences</u> often sound <u>jumbled up</u>.

<u>Don't give up</u> right away — you just need to <u>practise</u> reading it. The <u>more</u> you <u>read</u> the play, the <u>easier</u> it'll get to <u>understand</u>.

A famous chicken insult — Hen-ry V...

<u>Understanding</u> the play — that's the hardest part. The <u>more</u> you read it, the <u>easier</u> it'll get. And that means you'll do <u>better</u> in your SAT. It's up to you — if you <u>stick at it</u> you'll get <u>good marks</u>.

2

Section One — Henry V: The Story

What Happens In The Play

If you want good marks in your Paper 2, you've got to know the play well. You need to know what happens and why it happens. If you've already read the play, use these two pages to revise.

The Main Story is King Henry's Invasion of France

1) Henry has just become King of England. Everybody is amazed by how wise and religious he is, because he used to be a real tearaway. King Henry wants to take a lot of money from the Church. To distract him, the Archbishop of Canterbury tells Henry he's got a claim to be King of France. Henry decides to invade.

I'm going to take wads of cash from the Church.

I think you'll find that's "I'm going to invade France"

This isn't the Caribbean cruise we booked...

I feel sick...

Where's France?

2) Meanwhile the son of the French king, the Dauphin, sends tennis balls to Henry as a joke — saying he's a child who's only fit for games. Henry's furious and swears he'll get his revenge. Three traitors, bribed by the French, plot to kill King Henry — he uncovers the plot in time and they are executed. Henry and his army sail for France.

3) After a siege, Henry captures the French city of Harfleur. The French King sends an army to fight Henry, who's trying to get to Calais. Henry's army are sick and starving, and the French outnumber them 5 to 1. The night before the battle, Henry goes through the English camp in disguise and talks to some of his men. Next day he makes a brilliant speech to his men encouraging them to be brave. The leaders of the French army are sure they'll beat the English.

Come on, lads, we'll win together!

YES!

4) The English army defeats the bigger French force at the Battle of Agincourt. At one stage, Henry is afraid that the French will reinforce their men and keep fighting. He orders the execution of all French prisoners. Some of the French attack and rob the English camp and kill all the boy servants. The French are defeated, and Henry goes back to England in triumph.

5) King Henry makes peace with the French on two conditions. He marries the King of France's daughter, and becomes his heir — when the French King dies, Henry will become King of France too. The Chorus reminds us that Henry died soon after, but his son became King of France and England.

There are Also Two Dodgy Comedy Plots

1) Bardolph, Pistol and Nym are three dodgy characters who join Henry's army. Bardolph and Pistol are Henry's old drinking friends. They make lots of jokes and act like cowards.

2) Bardolph and Nym both get hanged for stealing, and Pistol insults a Welsh captain, Llewellyn, who forces him to eat a leek as punishment.

1) When Henry's in disguise, he has an argument with a soldier called Michael Williams. They swap gloves as a promise to settle their quarrel later.

2) After the battle, Henry tells Llewellyn to look out for a traitor who carries a certain glove. Llewellyn spots the glove and accuses Williams of being a traitor. Henry pardons Williams for the quarrel and gives him a gift of gold coins.

Dodgy haircut stories — another comb-edy plot...

Blimey — there's a lot going on this play. First things first, make sure you get the main story straight in your mind. You need to know the order things happen in. Then look at the comedy plots.

What You've Got to Do

The <u>whole play</u> sounds pretty long and complicated — but <u>don't</u> worry about that.
<u>All you've got to do</u> in your SAT is read <u>one short bit</u> from the play and do <u>one task</u> based on it.

You've Got to Do One Task in Your SAT

There'll be six tasks about Shakespeare plays in your SAT paper — you only have
to do one of them. <u>Only two</u> tasks are about <u>Henry V</u>. Ignore the rest.

You only need one mask...

No, I think it's "task"

The <u>tasks</u> are <u>questions</u> that ask you to <u>write something</u> about <u>part</u>
of the play. You get <u>loads</u> of <u>hints</u> to help you with your answer.

Each Task has a Bit of the Play that Goes with It

1) Each task is about one particular <u>bit</u> of the play, and it'll tell you <u>exactly</u> which bit. For example:

| Act 2 Scene 2 | <u>or</u> | Act 5 Scene 2, line 98 to the end of the scene |

2) As well as the question paper, you'll get a <u>booklet</u> with all the different bits of the plays.
Find the bits from <u>Henry V</u>. Don't even <u>look</u> at any of the other plays.

Read Both Tasks Through

There are lots of <u>different tasks</u> you could be asked to do. Read both tasks through and check
<u>which scene</u> they ask about. You'll <u>definitely</u> have studied at least <u>one</u> of the scenes in class.

This tells you which play
the task is about... ➡ **Henry V**

...And this tells you
which bit of the play. ➡ **Act 4 Scene 1**

This sets the scene — it's here to
tell you what's happening. **TASK 1**

In this scene King Henry goes through the English Camp in disguise
and meets Williams, Court and Bates.

What do we learn about the character of King Henry in this scene?

Here's the actual task — you've got to answer <u>this question</u>.

Before you begin to write you should think about:

You'll also get a sentence like this, followed by
some <u>handy tips</u> for answering the question.
They're there to <u>help you</u> — so <u>use</u> them all.

that's tips, not lips...

English Camp — Carry On Henry V, perhaps...

You've only got to answer <u>one</u> question in your Shakespeare SAT. That means it's <u>dead important</u> to
pick a task about a scene you <u>know</u> really <u>well</u>. Read the questions <u>carefully</u> before you choose.

How to Get Good Marks

This is mega-important. You've got to do <u>all</u> of this in your SAT — so get it clear in your head now.

You've Got to *Show* You *Understand the Scene*

<u>This</u> is the secret of doing well in Paper 2 — <u>understanding the scene</u> you're writing about. It's what you're going to be <u>marked</u> on.

Now I understand the bean!

BEANS   NOT BEANS

① *Show You Know What Happens*

> What do we learn about the character of King Henry in this scene?

Write about what <u>he says</u>, what <u>he does</u>, and what the <u>other</u> characters <u>say</u> about <u>him</u>.

You <u>can't</u> write a <u>good</u> answer <u>unless</u> you know exactly <u>what happens</u> in the scene.

② *Show You Know What the Characters are Like*

...and I know what the carrot-ears are like.

King Henry seems very confident when he is speaking to the nobles, Erpingham, Bedford and Gloucester. Even when he is in disguise, he tells Williams, Court and Bates that he is right — "his cause being just and his quarrel honourable." (Act 4, Scene 1, lines 126-7)

You have to find bits in the scenes to <u>back up</u> what you're saying. You need to <u>prove</u> you <u>know</u> what you're <u>talking about</u>.

③ *Write about the Mood of the Scene*

Say what it <u>feels like</u> to hear or read the scene. Find the <u>exact bits</u> of Shakespeare's language that make you feel like that, and <u>write it down</u>. This sounds tricky — all it really means is <u>thinking carefully</u> about what the scene makes you <u>feel</u>.

I feel silly.

This scene feels strange, because the audience recognises the King, but Williams doesn't. When Williams criticises the King, he's actually doing it to his face. Henry says he heard the King refusing to be ransomed. Williams answers him bitterly: "Ay, he said so, to make us fight cheerfully;" (line 192). It makes you wonder whether Henry's confidence is real, or just another trick.

A lot of things in the play seem pretty <u>strange</u> to us — but Section 3 has plenty of useful <u>background bits</u> that'll <u>help</u> you understand it.

How to understand the seen — open your eyes...

Understanding the scene — <u>that's</u> what it's all about. You have to show the examiners that you know <u>what happens</u> in the scene, and what the <u>characters</u> are like — look at Sections 5 and 6.

Writing Well & Giving Examples

Two more <u>key things</u> you have to do here — make sure you stick them away in your brainbox.

You Also Get Marked on <u>How Well You Write</u>

1) It's harsh but true — you've got to get your <u>spelling</u> and <u>punctuation</u> perfect. They'll <u>take marks away</u> from you if you don't.

2) Don't forget to write in <u>paragraphs</u>. Every time you want to talk about a <u>new idea</u>, start a <u>new paragraph</u>.

3) Here's the <u>tough</u> one — try to sound <u>interested</u> in the play, even if you don't like it. Show the examiners that you're keen by using lots of <u>interesting words</u> and <u>phrases</u> in your answer.

This is tricky...

How a Well Writes

> *Shakespeare makes the scene comic by his brilliant use of over-the-top heroic language — it makes Pistol sound ridiculous.*

You've Got to Give <u>Loads of</u> Examples

They want you to give <u>examples</u> from the scene that have <u>something</u> to do with the task you chose. For a <u>really good</u> answer, you need to <u>explain why</u> your examples are relevant.

> Don't make your examples <u>too long</u>. <u>Two lines</u> is about right.

Examples Examples Examples

You Can Write about Any <u>Versions</u> of the Play You've Seen

In your answer, you can write about <u>any versions</u> of the play you've seen. Be careful, though. You <u>won't</u> get extra marks just because you've seen the play. <u>Only</u> write about a production you've seen if it actually <u>helps</u> you <u>answer the question</u>. Don't wander off the point.

Every version has a <u>director</u> who decides what the <u>costumes</u> will look like, which <u>actors</u> will play the characters and how they'll <u>say their lines</u>.

Some directors <u>change</u> loads of things in the play. Any version <u>you've</u> seen is only <u>one way</u> of doing it.

We're doing it as Henry V, King of Surfers.

Yeah, like, "Once more on to the beach, my friends"

Er, you can't go changing the words

There are two really famous <u>films</u> of <u>Henry V</u>. One stars Laurence Olivier, who directed it as well. His version shows Henry as a <u>great hero</u> — it was made in 1944 during the Second World War.

The other version stars Kenneth Branagh, who was the director too. His version is much darker, showing Henry's <u>doubts</u> and <u>fears</u>, and making the <u>battle scenes</u> really horrible and <u>realistic</u>.

Shakespeare plays — scene and not heard...

You're being marked on <u>two</u> things in your SAT — how well you <u>read</u> and <u>understand</u> the bit from the play and how well you <u>write</u> about it. And the secret is to give plenty of <u>examples</u>.

Revision Summary

This second section's here to give you a nice big chunk of knowledge about <u>Henry V</u>, and about how to do well at the SAT tasks. It won't do you much good if you don't learn it, though. This is where these cunning Revision Summary questions come in. Do them all, don't miss any out, and keep going until you're sure you've got every last one of the blighters right. If you don't know the answers at first, find the right page and go over it again. Then have another go...

1) What's the main story of <u>Henry V</u>?

2) Why does Henry invade France?

3) What is the title of the son of the French King?

4) Why does he send Henry some tennis balls?

5) What's the name of the French city Henry captures after a siege?

6) Where is Henry trying to get to when the French army is sent out?

7) By how many do the French army outnumber the English?

8) What does Henry do the night before the battle?

9) What does Henry do the next day?

10) How do the French army feel before the battle?

11) What is the name of the battle?

12) What does Henry order when he is afraid the French will reinforce their men?

13) What do some of the French do to the English camp and the boy servants?

14) Who wins the battle, the French or the English?

15) What does Henry do after the battle?

16) What two conditions does Henry make before he agrees to make peace with France?

17) In the SAT, how many questions will there be about <u>Henry V</u>?

18) How many questions do you have to answer?   a) *One*   b) *Two*   c) *As many as you like.*

19) If the task gives you four hints to think about before you start to write, how many of the hints should you write about?   a) *None of them — they're only hints*   b) *One or two, just to show you care*   c) *All four of them.*

20) What are the three key things you need to do to get good marks?

21) Apart from understanding the scene, what else do you get marked on?

22) If you've seen a film or a stage production of <u>Henry V</u>, are you allowed to write about it in the SAT?

Why the Play Seems Strange

Henry V is a strange play. It <u>doesn't</u> fit into the normal stereotypes of plays, because it's got a bit of <u>everything</u>. Make sure you understand <u>why</u> by getting all of this stuff <u>clear</u> in your mind.

Henry V is a History Play

Now this is pretty confusing. A <u>history play</u> is one that is <u>based</u> on English history.
It <u>doesn't</u> mean that it's <u>actually</u> what happened in the past — it's just a <u>story</u> based on real life.

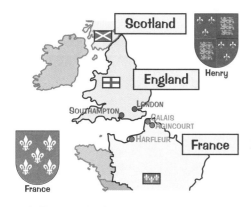

1) History plays were really <u>popular</u> in Shakespeare's time, especially ones that showed England <u>defeating</u> her enemies abroad. _Henry V_ is about a great <u>hero king</u> who <u>beats</u> the French in a famous battle.

2) Shakespeare wrote _Henry V_ in 1599. It was the <u>last</u> part of a <u>massive series</u> of history plays he wrote during the 1590s.

3) He'd already written _Henry VI Parts 1-3_, and _Richard III_ ages before, and he'd just done _Richard II_, and _Henry IV Parts 1-2_. _Henry V_ was the <u>climax</u> of his series, when the English were on <u>top</u> of the world.

It's a Mixture of Loads of Different Styles

Henry V has got a bit of everything. There's lots of <u>politics</u> and bits with nobles, but there are also some <u>comedy bits</u> with the <u>soldiers</u> in Henry's army. There's even a sort of <u>love-story</u>, where Henry gets to <u>chat up</u> the King of France's daughter. And don't forget the <u>battle</u> bits.

It's Over 400 Years Old too

A lot of _Henry V_ is pretty <u>weird</u> when you read it — but remember how <u>old</u> it actually is. It's like an episode of Eastenders <u>still</u> being popular in the year 2400. It's not surprising so much of it seems <u>strange</u> nowadays.

Blimey, now that <u>is</u> old!

It's Meant to be Acted — Not Just Read

"For oaths are straws, mens faiths are wafer cakes"? I've got a straw, but where's my cake?

1) _Henry V_ is a play, <u>not</u> a book — it's meant to be seen on a <u>stage</u> with <u>actors</u> playing the parts.

2) When you read it, all you get is what the characters <u>say</u>. It's often pretty hard to <u>follow</u> what's going on.

3) It makes more sense if you <u>imagine</u> what's happening. Think about what the characters are <u>like</u>, and how you think they would <u>speak</u> and <u>act</u>.

4) If you can, watch a <u>film or TV version</u> of the play. It's a great way to bring it to life — and you're allowed to <u>write about it</u> in your SAT, as long as it <u>fits in</u> with the question.

Plays about ancient snakes — hiss-story plays...

Henry V is a <u>history play</u> written to be <u>acted</u> — don't forget, that <u>doesn't</u> mean it's actually true.

Basic Play Stuff

This is going to sound really obvious but it's actually dead <u>important</u> — a lot of the weird things in <u>Henry V</u> simply come from the fact that it's a <u>play</u>.

The Play's Meant to be Watched by an Audience

I <u>still</u> can't see the play.

The whole point of a play is it <u>tells a story</u> by <u>showing you</u> what happened. You don't just hear the words — you see people talking and fighting. Anybody <u>watching</u> the play is part of the <u>audience</u>.

In your SAT, you'll get questions about how the <u>audience</u> is supposed to <u>feel</u>, or even about how <u>you</u> would <u>direct</u> a bit of the play.

It's Divided into Acts and Scenes

1) The play is divided into <u>five</u> big sections, called <u>acts</u>. Each act is like an <u>episode</u> of a TV serial — lots of things happen in it, but it's only <u>part</u> of the whole thing.

Henry V
Episode 10
The One Where Kate Has An English Lesson

2) Each act is made up of <u>smaller</u> sections called <u>scenes</u>. There's nothing complicated about them. A scene shows you a <u>small bit</u> of the story and then ends. Then a <u>new scene</u> starts that shows you the <u>next bit</u>.

3) Scenes are just a way of <u>breaking up</u> the story. They show that time has passed in the story — <u>one scene</u> could be set in the <u>evening</u> and the <u>next one</u> on the <u>following day</u>.

This play's going places

4) They also let the play <u>move</u> to <u>different places</u> — one scene will happen at the French Court, another scene will happen <u>somewhere else</u> in France.

In your SAT, you'll <u>only</u> have to read <u>one or two</u> scenes from the play.

Remember the Difference between Characters and Actors

It sounds a bit silly to say it — but every year people get <u>confused</u> between the characters and the actors. Get it straight — <u>characters</u> are the people <u>in</u> the story, like King Henry, Pistol etc. The <u>actors</u> are the people who <u>play them</u> on the stage or in a film. <u>Don't</u> get them muddled up.

King Henry is a <u>character</u>. Kenneth Branagh is an <u>actor</u> who played King Henry.

The difference between characters & actors — char & e...

All of this stuff <u>doesn't</u> really seem that tricky — but people keep getting it <u>wrong</u>. Don't be a dilbert, use your noodle and sort it out <u>now</u>, once and for all — <u>acts</u> and <u>scenes</u>, <u>characters</u> and <u>actors</u>, the whole nine yards. Believe me, once you <u>do</u> know it, you really are well on the way.

Tricky Play Stuff

Henry V has a few <u>special features</u> because it's a <u>history</u> play — and a few other features that turn up in pretty much any old Shakespeare play. Learn them <u>now</u> so they <u>don't</u> catch you out.

The Chorus is a Kind of Storyteller

Hi, there.

1) Before <u>each Act</u> in *Henry V*, there is a <u>speech</u> by somebody called the <u>Chorus</u>. He also has a speech right at the <u>beginning</u> of the play, and one at the very <u>end</u>.

Did someone say "huge bottom"?

2) These speeches are there to <u>set</u> the <u>scene</u>. They tell you <u>where</u> the action is and give you a <u>picture</u> of the whole scene — especially if it's something that <u>can't</u> properly be shown on a stage, like the English fleet crossing to France.

> behold the threaden sails,
> Borne with th'invisible and creeping wind,
> Draw the huge bottoms through the furrowed sea,
> Act 3, Chorus, 10-12

3) The Chorus also <u>apologises</u> for the fact you <u>can't</u> see these great battles or fleets onstage. Instead, he asks the audience to <u>fill in</u> the gaps with their <u>imaginations</u>. All the way through, he keeps reminding us to see the scenes in our <u>mind's eye</u>, using lots of <u>poetic descriptions</u>.

> For 'tis your thoughts that now must deck our kings,
> Prologue, 28

The Chorus apologises because there are only a <u>few actors</u> in <u>poor costumes</u> — it's all about <u>pretending</u>.

4) The Chorus can be a man <u>or</u> a woman. Some directors put the Chorus in <u>modern</u> clothes, <u>even</u> if the rest of the cast are in <u>old costumes</u>. All the Chorus' speeches are in poetry (see Section 4).

Sometimes Characters Talk to Themselves

When Shakespeare wants to show what a <u>character</u> is <u>thinking</u>, the character <u>talks to himself</u> or to the <u>audience</u>. It can <u>seem</u> a bit strange, but it's the <u>easiest</u> way to <u>show</u> you what's going on in their <u>mind</u>. <u>King Henry</u> does it in Act 4, Scene 1, and <u>Pistol</u> does it in Act 5, Scene 1.

Stage Directions Say What the Characters are Doing

Stage directions are little phrases in <u>brackets</u>, like these. <u>No one</u> actually <u>says</u> them.

Enter = when someone comes <u>onto</u> the stage.

Exit = when <u>one</u> person <u>leaves</u> the stage.

Exeunt = when <u>more than one</u> person leaves the stage.

Aside = to show a character's talking to <u>himself</u> or <u>herself</u>.

Alarum (or Alarm) = sound of <u>trumpet</u> or <u>drums</u> to signal a <u>battle</u> from offstage.

Tucket = a short <u>trumpet</u> flourish.

Parley = a trumpet call to <u>stop</u> the <u>fighting</u> and open <u>peace talks</u>.

Huge bottoms, eh — once more into the breeches...

Make sure you <u>know</u> what the <u>Chorus</u> does, and <u>learn</u> all of these useful <u>stage direction</u> words.

Key Facts about the Play

Henry V is all about what it <u>means</u> to be a <u>King</u> — blimey, that sounds a bit scary.
This page of <u>key background</u> stuff should help you <u>work out</u> what that means.

Henry V was a *Popular* and *Patriotic* Play

1) In 1590s England, history plays were really popular. In 1588, the Spanish Armada
had been <u>defeated</u>, so audiences <u>loved</u> to see plays about great <u>English victories</u>.

E-N-G-L-A-N-D!
Go England!

2) The <u>historical</u> King Henry V was seen as the <u>ideal</u> king — a great <u>war hero</u>
who never gave up, but sadly <u>died</u> when he was quite young. In a lot of
stories, Henry had been a <u>lazy rebel</u> when he was <u>younger</u>. When he
became King, he suddenly <u>grew up</u> and became a <u>good</u> and <u>noble</u> leader.

3) Shakespeare wrote his play *Henry V* at the end of his huge <u>cycle</u> of
history plays, as the <u>climax</u> of the story — the <u>golden age</u> of
England. He had <u>already</u> written about Henry as an <u>idle young</u>
<u>prince</u>. Now he was writing about him as a <u>king</u> and a <u>hero</u>.

There are *Two Main Ways* of *Looking at the Play*

① Some people say *Henry V* is a <u>propaganda</u> play. It's all about
how <u>great</u> King Henry is and how <u>fantastic</u> all his victories are.

② Other people say it's an <u>attack</u> on the King — because he is shown to
be <u>ruthless</u> and <u>cruel</u>. Even though he wins, the war is a <u>waste</u> of the
<u>lives</u> of all the <u>ordinary soldiers</u> who got killed. It's all about Henry's
<u>selfish ambition</u> to be the King of France, and to win <u>more power</u>.

<u>These views</u> are completely <u>opposite</u> — make up <u>your own</u>
<u>mind</u> by looking for <u>evidence</u> of <u>both views</u> in the play.

The Play's *Based* on *Several* *Different Sources*

Shakespeare used <u>three main sources</u> for his play: Holinshed's *Third Volume of Chronicles*
(1587), Hall's *The Union of the Noble and Illustre Families of Lancaster and York* (1548)
and an anonymous play from the 1580s called *The Famous Victories of Henry V*.

The <u>real</u> Henry V fought in France on <u>three separate occasions</u>. He won the <u>Battle of</u>
<u>Agincourt</u> in <u>1415</u>, but <u>didn't</u> make peace with the French until <u>1420</u>. In the <u>play</u>, the Battle
happens in Act 4, and the Treaty happens in Act 5 — so it's <u>not</u> very historically accurate.

Henry <u>married</u> Katherine of France and had a son, but <u>died</u> in 1422, leaving the baby <u>Henry VI</u>
to become <u>King of England</u> and later of <u>France</u> — but during his reign, <u>all</u> of his father's conquests
were <u>lost</u>. Shakespeare <u>tells us</u> that this will happen, right at the end of the play, in the <u>Epilogue</u>.

Shakespeare's favourite historical source — HP or HV...

Good news — you <u>don't</u> need to know all this stuff <u>off by heart</u>. It's here to help you <u>understand</u>
the play <u>better</u> when you read it. Just remember the <u>two main ways</u> of <u>looking</u> at the <u>play</u>.

Kings

Medieval and Elizabethan Kings were pretty powerful people. They could do whatever they wanted — which is why Shakespeare thought they were interesting to write about.

Strong Kings Could Do Whatever They Wanted

Haystacks thought that he should definitely be the next king.

1) The King was the head of society. It was his job to run the government and to control all the barons and nobles. A strong King could control them, and would organise the country to do exactly what he wanted.

2) Problems came when there was a weak King. Then the barons would try to tell him what to do — or even plot to kill the King, like Scroop, Gray and Cambridge do in Act 2, Scene 2 of the play.

3) Everyone wanted a strong ruler for the country. When there wasn't one, the barons would fight and the country would be caught up in civil war. That's exactly what happened in Henry VI's reign.

4) It had also happened in the reign of Richard II — Henry V's father had taken over from him as King, even though he wasn't really the rightful heir. Henry's father felt guilty about this (Shakespeare shows it in _Henry IV, Parts 1-2_). Shakespeare shows Henry V still feeling guilty about his father stealing the throne, because he mentions it in his prayer in Act 4, Scene 1.

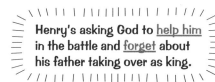

Henry's asking God to help him in the battle and forget about his father taking over as king.

O not today, think not upon the fault
My father made in compassing the crown.
Act 4, Scene 1, 276-7

The King is Responsible for Everything

Being the King means people hold Henry responsible for everything. When he goes around the camp in disguise, some ordinary soldiers tell him what they think of the war.

...we know enough if we know we are the King's subjects. If his cause be wrong, our obedience to the King wipes the crime of it out of us.
Act 4, Scene 1, 122-5

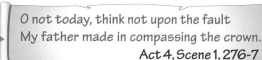

It's all your fault!

Sigh... It's a hard life...

They're saying that they only fight because they're obeying the king. If King Henry is fighting for the wrong reason, then it's his fault not theirs.

Henry himself tells us that his people blame him for things that aren't his fault. He also has to make lots of hard decisions. That's what it means to be King and it isn't easy.

During the play, Henry has to make some tough decisions. He threatens all sorts of horrible things to make the Governor of Harfleur surrender in Act 3, Scene 4. In Act 3, Scene 7, he accepts that his old friend Bardolph has to be hanged. In Act 4, Scene 5, he orders his men to kill all the French prisoners.

We must bear all.
Act 4, Scene 1, 230

Henry's the king — I thought that was Elvis...

Hmmm — being a King isn't as much of a laugh as you might think. In the play, Henry has to make lots of tough decisions, and take the responsibility for them. He gets blamed for lots of things too.

Warfare

Most of *Henry V* happens during a war — but the kind of war Shakespeare's on about is pretty different from a modern war. This page could come in handy for answering the SAT tasks.

Wars were about Politics and Money

1) In *Henry V*, the war is all about who's the rightful King of France. In Act 1, Scene 2, the Archbishop of Canterbury tells King Henry that he has a lawful claim to be King of France, and encourages him to start a war with the French King.

2) The Archbishop does this because Henry wants to take money and land away from the Church — he's trying to get Henry interested in something else.

3) The Dauphin, the French King's son, sends tennis balls to Henry as an insult — saying he's a child only fit for games. This makes Henry even more determined to invade. The Dauphin is the rightful heir to the French throne, so he's all for fighting Henry as soon as possible. However, the French King is cautious.

4) Aside from the politics, wars were a great way to make money. Armies used to steal supplies and treasure from the places they attacked. In *Henry V*, the King makes clear rules for the English army to stop them stealing, because he doesn't want the French to hate him:

NO STEALING!
NO SWEARING!

> ...we give express charge that in our marches through the country there be nothing compelled from the villages, nothing taken but paid for, none of the French upbraided or abused in disdainful language...
> Act 3 Scene 7, 99-102

5) In battle, soldiers could make money by capturing nobles from the other army and demanding a ransom to let them go. Pistol does just that in Act 4, Scene 4 of the play. Soldiers of the winning army would also take money and clothes from the dead bodies on the battlefield — it was seen as the rightful prize of the army.

> And my poor soldiers tell me yet ere night
> They'll be in fresher robes, or they will pluck
> The gay new coats o'er the French soldiers' heads
> Act 4, Scene 3, 117-119

Here King Henry's telling the French Herald that although his soldiers look rough now, by nightfall they'll be dead or wearing the robes of the dead French soldiers.

Henry's Army is a Mix of Nobles and Common Men

The English Army is a mix of nobles, professional soldiers and ordinary people who've signed up to fight. There would also be butlers, bakers, blacksmiths and servants like the Boy.

Pistol, Bardolph and Nym join the army to make a profit out of the war. They don't care about being heroes, just about making money and not getting hurt or killed.

> For I shall sutler be unto the camp, and profits will accrue.
> Act 2, Scene 1, 88-9

Pistol says he'll be a sutler. Sutlers sold food to the soldiers.

Henry's army — at the end of his shouldery...

The war in the play is all about Henry wanting to be King of France — but it's also about money. Keep in mind that Pistol, Nym and Bardolph are out for a profit, and how important ransoms were.

Some Key Themes

Henry V is <u>odd</u> because the audience actually <u>know</u> the story right from the start. You <u>don't</u> watch to see <u>what</u> happens, but <u>how</u> it happens — what <u>themes</u> the play looks at along the way.

The <u>Rules</u> of War are <u>Changing</u>

"The Rules of Fighting" proved to be a very useful book for Bill and Geoff.

1) Henry's army is involved in <u>two</u> major battles — the <u>siege of Harfleur</u> and the <u>Battle of Agincourt</u>.

2) At the siege, the English use <u>cannons</u> and <u>mines</u> to attack the city. Mines were <u>tunnels</u> dug by the soldiers under the <u>city walls</u>, where they could put <u>explosives</u> to try to make a <u>breach</u> — a hole in the wall.

3) In <u>Act 3, Scene 3</u>, Llewellyn and Macmorris <u>argue</u> about whether these new tactics <u>should</u> be used in war at all.

4) At the <u>real</u> Battle of Agincourt, the English won because they used <u>longbowmen</u> protected by <u>wooden stakes</u>. The French cavalry <u>couldn't</u> get near them — a longbow shot could <u>pierce</u> full armour from 250 metres away.

5) <u>None</u> of this happens in the play. Instead, the English <u>win</u> because of <u>King Henry's big speech</u> in <u>Act 4, Scene 3</u>, where he <u>inspires</u> his men to fight bravely (see bottom of page).

King Henry <u>Breaks</u> the <u>Rules</u> of War

I've broken your ruler. What are you going to do about it?

Hey!

Craig's ruler fight got off to a bad start when Lucy broke the ruler of war.

He's supposed to be <u>ruthless</u> and <u>fair</u>, because it's part of being King — but in <u>Act 4, Scene 6</u> the French Army <u>come back</u> to the battle, and he orders his men to <u>kill</u> all the French <u>prisoners</u>.

> Then every soldier kill his prisoners.
> Act 4, Scene 6, 37

Some people say that Henry is a <u>war criminal</u>.

This is completely <u>against</u> the rules of war — soldiers surrendered because they thought they would be <u>ransomed</u>. It also means that all Henry's soldiers, including Pistol, <u>lose</u> the ransom money they <u>thought</u> they'd won.

In <u>Act 4, Scene 7</u>, you find out that the French have <u>attacked</u> the English camp and <u>killed</u> all the <u>servant boys</u>. This was also <u>against</u> the rules of war — the English captain Gower says that this is <u>why</u> Henry had the prisoners killed. In fact, he had them killed <u>before</u> the attack on the camp.

But Henry Manages to <u>Unite</u> His <u>Army</u>

In <u>Act 3</u>, you can see the <u>divisions</u> in the English and French armies. Before Harfleur, in <u>Scenes 2 and 3</u>, you see the English soldiers <u>arguing</u> among themselves. The <u>French nobles</u> are shown squabbling over petty things in <u>Scene 8</u>.

Even in <u>Act 4, Scene 1</u>, the disguised Henry <u>argues</u> with Williams, Court and Bates about whether the King's cause is <u>just</u>.

But in <u>Act 4, Scene 3</u>, Henry <u>speaks</u> to his soldiers <u>directly</u>. He says that they're all <u>equal</u>, a <u>band of brothers</u> on the battlefield. This is <u>why</u> the English <u>win</u> — because they're <u>united</u>, and the French are <u>divided</u>.

Your explosive tunnel — I think it's mine...

Make up your own mind — a <u>war criminal</u> or a <u>ruthless hero</u> who <u>unites</u> his army against the odds.

Problems with the Play

Watch out — this page is dead <u>important</u>. There are some <u>big problems</u> with <u>*Henry V*</u> that you need to know about, if you <u>don't</u> want to get <u>caught out</u> by anything in your SAT.

Henry's **Character Is** Strange **and** Unlikeable

1) A lot of people <u>don't</u> find Henry very interesting. You <u>don't</u> get to <u>see inside</u> his mind except in <u>Act 4, Scene 1</u>. The rest of the time you have to <u>work out</u> what he's thinking.

2) He is very <u>ruthless</u> and <u>unlikeable</u>. His <u>threats</u> at Harfleur are very extreme. His treatment of Bardolph's execution makes sense in the circumstances, though. His order to <u>kill</u> the French prisoners is so <u>controversial</u> that <u>both film versions</u> of the play <u>leave it out</u>.

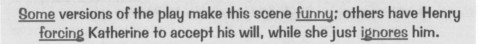

You all hate me, don't you?

3) His <u>marriage</u> to Katherine is completely <u>forced</u>. She is <u>made</u> to marry him by her father. That makes Act 5, Scene 2 very <u>strange</u>, where Henry tries to <u>chat her up</u>. It's supposed to be a scene where Henry shows his romantic <u>charm</u>, but it's pretty <u>pointless</u> if Katherine has <u>no real choice</u> in the matter.

> <u>Some</u> versions of the play make this scene <u>funny</u>; others have Henry <u>forcing</u> Katherine to accept his will, while she just <u>ignores</u> him.

4) Before Agincourt, King Henry <u>promises equality</u> to his soldiers. After the battle it <u>doesn't</u> happen. When he reads the list of English dead, he <u>only</u> names the <u>nobles</u>, not the <u>ordinary men</u>.

The Humour **in the Play** isn't **Very** Funny

But how's it going to play in Wales, Will?

Most of the <u>jokes</u> in the play come from the comic characters, Pistol, Bardolph and Nym, and the comedy Welshman, Llewellyn. Bardolph, Pistol and Nym are <u>cowardly thieves</u>. They speak in <u>comic ways</u> and <u>argue</u> a lot, but really they <u>aren't</u> that funny.

Llewellyn is made to be funny because of his comic <u>Welsh accent</u>, and his <u>obsession</u> with <u>ancient history</u> — he compares Henry to Alexander the Great, an ancient hero. The play also feature a <u>Scotsman</u> and an <u>Irishman</u>, who also have <u>comic accents</u>.

King Henry also plays <u>three tricks</u> in the play:

1) He tricks the <u>traitors</u>, Scroop, Gray and Cambridge into believing he <u>doesn't know</u> about their plot.
2) He <u>disguises himself</u> to go through the English camp before the battle, but ends up <u>arguing</u> with Bates, Williams and Court.
3) Finally, he plays a trick on <u>Llewellyn</u> and <u>Williams</u>, making them <u>challenge</u> each other to a duel. Some versions of the play make these tricks <u>funny</u>, <u>others</u> use them to show how Henry <u>manipulates</u> people selfishly.

Tee hee...

Things Aren't **what They** Appear **to be**

One of the <u>key ideas</u> in the play is that <u>appearances</u> can be deceiving. Don't take everything at face value. You need to keep your eyes open for <u>hidden meanings</u> in your SAT scene.

How insects look — their appear-ants...

<u>Henry's character</u>; whether it's <u>funny</u>; and <u>hidden meanings</u> — <u>look out</u> for these in your SAT scene.

Revision Summary

That's a relief — this section's finally over. Well, almost. Here's a page of questions to make sure you've got the important bits from this section safely tucked away in your brains. Get this stuff learned and work your way through these questions. If you can't do them, go back over the right pages and have another go. That's the key to understanding the play — making sure you know the facts. If you want to do well, that's what you've got to do — it's your choice...

1) What is a history play?

2) When was *Henry V* written?

3) Is it just meant to be read? If not, what else is it supposed to be?

4) What is the audience?

5) What's the play divided into? *a) days and weeks b) nights and days c) acts and scenes.*

6) What's the difference between characters and actors?

7) Who is the Chorus and what is his/her job?

8) Why do characters sometimes talk to themselves in the play?

9) Are the stage directions spoken or not?

10) What kind of King was Henry V seen as? *a) an idle King b) an ideal King c) an Irish King.*

11) What are the two main ways of looking at the play *Henry V*?

12) Is Shakespeare's *Henry V* an historically accurate play?

13) Why did everyone want a strong King?

14) Why does Henry feel guilty about his father in his prayer in Act 4, Scene 1?

15) What is the war in *Henry V* about?

16) How could soldiers make money out of the war?

17) How does King Henry break the rules of war?

18) Write down three of the problems with the play.

Henry V: An Idle King?

Why the Language is Hard

Everyone says Shakespeare's plays are brilliant, but they can be a <u>nightmare</u> to understand.
Here's the good news — <u>Henry V</u> <u>isn't</u> as hard as you might think... if you <u>read</u> this lot <u>carefully</u>.

Warning — *The* Language *Looks Really* Tricky

I wish he'd give me a proper look at the words.

The audience is getting restless...

1) Shakespeare's language looks <u>hard</u> — but there's <u>no way round it</u>, I'm afraid. You'll be given a <u>scene</u> to read in your SAT — and you've <u>got</u> to be able to <u>understand</u> what happens, or you won't get <u>any marks</u> at all.

2) The <u>best way</u> to work out the language is to <u>read</u> bits from the play <u>out loud</u> with a group of mates. You'll be surprised — stuff that made <u>no sense</u> on the page will actually start to <u>get clearer</u>.

3) Don't forget — it was <u>meant</u> to be spoken out loud. That's the way you're <u>supposed</u> to understand it — <u>don't</u> just sit and read it in your head.

There's <u>no point</u> in <u>worrying</u> about how hard it is
— just <u>get on</u> and <u>learn how</u> to <u>read</u> it.

Some *of the Play's in* Poetry *— Some* Isn't

<u>Henry V</u> is written in a mixture of <u>poetry</u> and <u>prose</u>.
Prose is just any kind of language that <u>isn't</u> poetry.

(1) Here's how to <u>spot</u> a bit of <u>poetry</u>.

<u>Every line</u> starts with a <u>capital letter</u>, even if it comes in the <u>middle</u> of a sentence.

> Thou dost thy office fairly. Turn thee back
> And tell thy king I do not seek him now.
> Act 3, Scene 7, 120-1

...and here's a bit of spottery up a tree.

<u>Sometimes</u> the last word of a line <u>rhymes</u> with the last word of the <u>next one</u>.

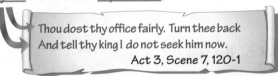

> Now forth, Lord Constable and Princes all
> And quickly bring us word of England's fall.
> Act 3, Scene 6, 67-8

(2) Any bits where the lines run on normally, <u>without</u> extra capitals or rhymes, are in <u>prose</u>.

> That's a lie in thy throat. I charge you in his majesty's name
> apprehend him, he's a friend of the Duke Alençon's.
> Act 4, Scene 8, 15-17

There's <u>no</u> capital letter.

A Tellytubby chewing plants poem — Po-ate-tree...

The secret of this language stuff is just <u>getting used</u> to it. It's never going to get any easier unless
you <u>read</u> the play lots. Sounds boring, I know, but it's the <u>only way</u> to <u>work out</u> what's going on.

Key Things To Look Out For

The <u>secret</u> of writing about Shakespeare's language is knowing <u>what</u> to <u>look out for</u>.
You <u>don't</u> have to understand every word — just keep your eyes open for a few <u>key things</u>.

Look at Whether King Henry Uses 'I' or 'We'

Henry <u>sometimes</u> talks about himself as '<u>I</u>' and <u>sometimes</u> as '<u>we</u>'.
That <u>isn't</u> because he was rubbish at grammar, though...

Henry uses '<u>we</u>' in <u>formal</u> and <u>public</u> scenes, such as the <u>Court</u> scenes. <u>All</u> Kings refer to themselves as 'we' and 'us' — it's called the <u>royal 'we'</u>. The <u>French King</u> does it too.

> We are no tyrant, but a Christian king,
> Act 1, Scene 2, 241

I know exactly who I am.

...of course we do.

Sometimes Henry uses 'I' and 'me' in the <u>middle</u> of one of these scenes. This is <u>important</u>, because it usually means he's giving his <u>personal opinion</u>.

Henry uses 'I' when he's <u>angry</u> — after the <u>Dauphin's insult</u>, and to his former friend Scroop after he's uncovered the <u>plot</u> against him.

> What shall I say to thee, Lord Scroop,
> Act 2, Scene 2, 91

When King Henry is told about Bardolph's execution, Henry uses 'we', <u>not</u> 'I'. He <u>avoids</u> giving a <u>personal</u> response, even though Bardolph <u>used</u> to be his friend. Instead he's being <u>ruthless</u> as a leader — he could be <u>hiding</u> his true feelings.

> We would have all such offenders so cut off,
> Act 3, Scene 7, 91

Always <u>check</u> whether Henry is using '<u>I</u>' or '<u>we</u>', and think about <u>why</u>.

In his big speech in <u>Act 4, Scene 3</u>, Henry uses 'we' to talk about the <u>whole army</u> and 'I' to talk about <u>himself</u>.

Watch Out for Old Words as well

Henry V was written 400 years ago — so <u>learn</u> this list of <u>common old words</u> in the play.
It'll <u>definitely</u> help you <u>understand</u> your SAT scene better.

is't = is it	didst = did	doth give/ doth limp	= gives/ limps
i'th' = in the	dost = do	yonder	= over there
'tis = it is	hath = has/ have	hither	= to here
a = I (sometimes)	wots = knows	coz	= cousin

Thou = You   Thee = You   Thy = Your

The characters use '<u>thou</u>', '<u>thee</u>' and '<u>thy</u>' when they're talking to <u>friends</u> or people they <u>know well</u>.

They also use them when they're talking to people of a <u>lower social class</u>, such as when Henry speaks to Williams.

Characters also use them when they're <u>insulting</u> someone, like Montjoy in his speeches to Henry.

Common old words — 'it wasn't like this in my day'...

Watch out for <u>when</u> Henry uses '<u>I or we</u>' — and get that list of <u>old words</u> into your <u>memory banks</u>.

How To Read The Poetry

It's a pain in the neck, but you've got to know how to read the poetry in the play.

The Poetry Always Has Ten or Eleven Syllables

Every line of poetry in the play has got ten or eleven syllables — or beats.

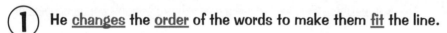

| 1 | 2 | 3 | 4 | 5 | 6 | 7 | 8 | 9 | 10 |

That fought with us upon Saint Crispin's day.

They give the poetry its rhythm.

This is what makes the poetry tricky to read — Shakespeare fiddles with the words to make them fit into lines of ten or eleven syllables with this rhythm.

① He changes the order of the words to make them fit the line.

ordering change

> I Richard's body have interrèd new,
> Act 4, Scene 1, 278

= I have interred (buried) Richard's body again.

② Sometimes he makes a word last for an extra syllable.

Normally "armed" has one syllable — but here you have to say it "arm - ed" so there are ten syllables in the line.

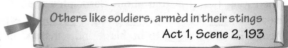

> Others like soldiers, armèd in their stings
> Act 1, Scene 2, 193

③ Worst of all, he even leaves whole words out — what a pain.

> The confident and over-lusty French
> Do the low-rated English play at dice,
> Act 4, Chorus, 18-19

"Do the low-rated English play at dice" doesn't seem to make any sense — it means "play at dice for the ransoms of the English soldiers."

Don't Stop Reading at the End of Each Line

1) Even though each line starts with a capital letter, it doesn't mean it's a separate sentence. Just ignore the capitals and follow the punctuation.

> Now entertain conjecture of a time
> When creeping murmur and the poring dark
> Fills the wide vessel of the universe
> Act 4, Chorus, 1-3

2) There's no full stop so carry on to the next line.

There'd better be a full stop soon.

3) There isn't a break in the sentence even when it moves to the next line. You've got to read it as if it's written like this:

"Now entertain conjecture of a time when creeping murmur and the poring dark fills the wide vessel of the universe."

My own syllable? — beats me...

Every line of poetry in the play has ten or eleven syllables — learn that and the rest'll start to follow.

Different Kinds Of Poetry

I can't say this is the most exciting stuff in the world — but it'll really <u>boost</u> your <u>marks</u>.
Some <u>SAT tasks</u> will ask you to talk about <u>how</u> Shakespeare <u>uses language</u>, so it's worth <u>learning</u>.

Most of the Play's in Blank Verse

It's a stupid name, blank verse — all it really means is any bits of poetry that <u>don't rhyme</u>.
The <u>only</u> thing that shows they're poetry is the number of <u>syllables</u> in each line
— yep, you've guessed it, <u>ten</u> or <u>eleven</u>.

> To be honest, I prefer plank verse.

Here's a line of blank verse.

> Where is the number of our English dead?
> Act 4, Scene 8, 96

This gets really hairy when <u>two people</u> are talking.
Their <u>conversation</u> has to <u>fit</u> into lines of poetry.

> KING HENRY   Who are the late commissioners?
> CAMBRIDGE   I one, my lord.
>   Your highness bade me ask for it today.
> SCROOP   So you did me, my liege.
> GRAY   And I, my royal sovereign.
>   Act 2, Scene 2, 61-3

These two bits form <u>one</u> line — that's why they're written like this.

<u>These two bits</u> together form <u>another</u> line.

Some Bits of it Rhyme

Some parts of the play have <u>bits</u> of rhyme in them — especially at the <u>end</u> of scenes.

> Cheerily to sea, the signs of war advance.
> No king of England if not king of France!
> Act 2, Scene 2, 190-91

jaw

claw

> Mowgli realised too late that he was running out of rhymes to amuse the hungry beast.

The Chorus Speaks in Poetry

All of the Chorus' speeches are in <u>poetry</u>. They're full of <u>powerful images</u> and <u>rich language</u> to make the beginning of each scene <u>come to life</u>.

> Think when we talk of horses that you see them
> Printing their proud hooves i'th' receiving earth,
> Prologue, 26-7

> Fire answers fire, and through their paly flames
> Each battle sees the other's umbered face.
> Act 4, Chorus, 8-9

Money for Shakespeare's old verse — a blank cheque...

It <u>isn't</u> just about Shakespeare writing poetry — it's about the <u>kinds of poetry</u> he uses in different scenes. You need to be able to <u>recognise</u> each kind so you can <u>write</u> about them in your SAT.

Why the Play's in Poetry & Prose

This is a mega-important bit. You need to learn why some parts of the play are in poetry and the others are in prose. It'll help you understand what's going on in each scene much better.

Shakespeare Uses Poetry for Formal or Serious Bits

All the serious and posh bits in *Henry V* tend to be in poetry.

1) Everyone speaks poetry in the scenes about politics in the English and French Courts. It shows the characters are talking about important things.

> Thus comes the English with full power upon us,
> And more than carefully it us concerns
> To answer royally in our defences.
>
> Act 2, Scene 4, 1-3

Dash it all, He's missed the ball!

2) King Henry always speaks in poetry when he's making public speeches or speaking to other English nobles.

> My lord of Warwick, and my brother Gloucester,
> Follow Llewellyn closely at the heels.
>
> Act 4, Scene 7, 159-60

3) The English nobles all speak poetry — and the French nobles do when they're making public speeches. In private, the French nobles speak prose.

He Uses Prose for Common Characters & Comedy Bits

All the ordinary characters in the play, like Bardolph, Nym, Llewellyn, Gower etc. speak prose. That doesn't stop them using some strange and fancy words, but they never speak poetry.

> BATES   I think it be. But we have no great cause to
>   desire the approach of day.
> WILLIAMS   We see yonder the beginning of day, but I think we
>   shall never see the end of it.
>
> Act 4, Scene 1, 84-87

In some editions of the play, Pistol's speeches are printed as poetry (see P.24 for more about Pistol's language).

Any comedy scenes in the play — like the trick Henry plays on Llewellyn and Williams — are in prose, usually because the ordinary characters are involved. One exception is the scene where the French nobles argue about silly things before the Battle of Agincourt.

pea-rose

> CONSTABLE   Tut, I have the best armour of
>   the world! Would it were day.
> ORLÉANS   You have excellent armour, but
>   let my horse have his due.
>
> Act 3, Scene 8, 1-4

King Henry speaks prose when he's talking to Llewellyn, and when he's in disguise talking to Williams, Court and Bates. He also speaks prose to Katherine in Act 5, Scene 2, to show he is a plain-speaking man as well as a powerful King.

Always check if a character is speaking poetry or prose in a scene — and think about why.

Shakespeare's language — from bad to verse...

Here's the deal — you've got to be able to give reasons why a scene uses poetry, prose or a mix.

Rhetoric

Henry V is a play with <u>lots</u> of <u>speeches</u>, which are all <u>packed</u> with <u>language tricks</u> to persuade people. That's what <u>rhetoric</u> means — <u>speechmaking tricks</u>. You'll need to know <u>all about</u> it.

Two Reasons Why People Make Speeches in the Play

1) When they want to <u>persuade</u> other characters about something. King Henry makes speeches in <u>Act 3, Scene 1</u> at the siege of Harfleur, and in <u>Act 4, Scene 3</u> before the Battle of Agincourt. He also uses <u>rhetoric</u> when he's talking to Katherine in <u>Act 5, Scene 2</u>.

2) Characters also make speeches to show they <u>won't</u> be <u>pushed around</u>: for example, when King Henry <u>replies</u> to the French Herald's <u>threats</u>.

perthauthive
th-peach

> <u>Speeches</u> can be in <u>prose</u> or <u>poetry</u>.

Learn to Spot these Four Speechmaking Tricks

(1) Look out for <u>rhetorical questions</u> — questions that <u>don't</u> expect an answer, or that the speaker <u>answers himself</u>.

> Show men dutiful?
> Why, so didst thou. Seem they grave and learnèd?
> Why, so didst thou. Come they of noble family?
> Why, so didst thou...
> Act 2, Scene 2, 127-30

> What's he that wishes so?
> My cousin, Westmorland. No my fair cousin
> Act 4, Scene 3, 18-19

(2) Keep 'em peeled for <u>alliteration</u> — <u>groups of words</u> in one or two lines that <u>start</u> with the <u>same letter</u>.

> I see you stand like greyhounds in the slips,
> Straining upon the start.
> Act 3, Scene 1, 31-2

(3) Check for <u>magic threes</u> — sentences with <u>three bits</u> that <u>go together</u>.

The <u>pauses between</u> each of the three bits give <u>extra stress</u> to each point.

> England shall repent his folly, see his weakness and admire our sufferance.
> Act 3, Scene 7, 114-15

> We few, we happy few, we band of brothers —
> Act 4, Scene 3, 60

Winston Churchill based his speeches during World War 2 on *Henry V.*

(4) See if you can spot <u>humour</u> or <u>exaggeration</u> in any speeches.

> But he'll remember, with advantages,
> What feats he did that day.
> Act 4, Scene 3, 51-2

This is a <u>joke</u>. King Henry's saying the soldiers will remember the battle but they'll <u>add extra bits</u> to the story to make themselves sound <u>more heroic</u>.

> Leaving their earthly parts to choke your clime,
> The smell whereof shall breed a plague in France.
> Act 4, Scene 3, 102-3

This is <u>exaggeration</u>. Henry says the English <u>dead</u> will <u>carry on</u> fighting the French by <u>rotting</u> and causing a <u>plague</u>.

Naming speeches — Rhett-or-Rick...

<u>Learn</u> this list of <u>speechmaking tricks</u> to look out for — and <u>why</u> characters make speeches anyway.

Understanding Pistol & the Hostess

The lowlife characters in the play turn up quite a bit — and a lot of what they say is seriously hard to work out, especially Pistol. This page'll help you get things a tad clearer.

Pistol's Language is all a Big Joke

Pistol's language in the play is often really tricky to understand. He uses all sorts of fancy images and long sentences.

> Bardolph, a soldier firm and sound of heart, and of buxom valour, hath by cruel fate and giddy Fortune's furious fickle wheel, that goddess blind that stands upon the rolling restless stone —
> Act 3, Scene 7, 24-7

No wonder I'm giddy. Let me off!

Shakespeare is making a big joke about the kind of language used in other people's plays at the time. They wrote strange and complicated poetry that sounded really artificial — no one ever spoke like that.

Shakespeare makes it a joke by having Pistol speak in this silly mix of poetry and prose. It's even funnier because Pistol speaks in this heroic language when he's really a huge coward. It's also comic for a rough and nasty character like Pistol to speak such fancy language.

Not everyone finds Pistol funny.

> I have, and I will hold the quondam Quickly for the only she, and pauca, there's enough.
> Act 2, Scene 1, 62-3

Quondam means 'once' or 'formerly' — ie his wife used to be called Quickly.

Watch out for repitition, like 'I have and I will hold', and alliteration, like the 'quondam Quickly', in Pistol's speeches.

Pistol's conversation with his French prisoner, Le Fer, in Act 4, Scene 4 is also ridiculous, because neither of them speak the other one's language. They end up misunderstanding each other until the Boy eventually translates.

> FRENCH   Oh, prenez miséricorde! Ayez pitié de moi!
> PISTOL   Moy shall not serve. I will have forty moys, or I will fetch thy rim out at thy throat, in drops of crimson blood.
> Act 4, Scene 4, 10-12

The Hostess Mixes Up Her Words

The Hostess only appears in two scenes of the play, but she ends up being quite funny because she keeps mixing up her words in stupid ways.

> BOY   Yes, that a did, and said they were devils incarnate.
> HOSTESS   A could never abide carnation, 'twas a colour he never liked.
> Act 2, Scene 3, 27-9

She muddles up incarnate ('made flesh') and carnation (a type of red) here.

Pistol — I'd play his part like a shot...

This stuff will really come in handy if you get asked to write about the language in any scene with Pistol in it. Just remember it's a joke — you don't have to understand every word to write about it.

Dialects & French

Phew — as if all this <u>old</u> and <u>fancy</u> language wasn't enough, there's tons of <u>French</u> in the play. And then there's loads of <u>dialect</u> stuff too — a Welshman, a Scotsman and an Irishman. Sounds like a bit of a joke to me...

There's Lots of French in the Play

Don't panic — they're <u>not</u> going to ask you to translate loads of <u>weird French</u>. <u>Most</u> of the French in the play comes in the <u>middle</u> of scenes in <u>English</u>. It's there to <u>remind</u> you that these characters are French.

> CONSTABLE O diable!
> ORLÉANS O Seigneur! Le jour est perdu, tout est perdu!
> Act 4, Scene 5, 1-2

Pierre's mother was strict about swearing.

In this bit, Shakespeare uses French because the nobles are <u>swearing</u> — they are saying the name of God in vain. The French nobles do this <u>all the time</u> in the play, showing that they are <u>less religious</u> than <u>King Henry</u>, who <u>never</u> swears.

> There's only <u>one whole scene</u> in French — <u>Act 3, Scene 5</u>, where Princess Katherine gets an <u>English lesson</u> from her servant Alice. If you <u>see</u> the play, you can <u>follow</u> this scene <u>just</u> from the way it is <u>acted</u> — you <u>don't</u> need to understand the French.

Llewellyn, Jamy and Macmorris Speak Dialects

Shakespeare tries to show <u>where</u> they come from in their <u>language</u>. He's trying to show all the different parts of Britain <u>united</u> in the play — even though it <u>wasn't</u> historically true.

In an emergency dial X.

<u>Llewellyn</u> uses '<u>p</u>' instead of '<u>b</u>' in some words, and says '<u>look you</u>' a lot of the time. He also uses the <u>wrong words</u> in some sentences. Shakespeare's audience would have found this <u>funny</u>.

> th'adversary was have possession of the pridge,
> Act 3, Scene 7, 85-6

> Captain Macmorris, when there is more better opportunity to be required, look you, I will be so bold as to tell you I know the disciplines of war, and there is an end.
> Act 3, Scene 3, 74-76

That <u>doesn't</u> mean he was just a joke — Shakespeare shows him to be one of the <u>bravest</u> of Henry's soldiers.

<u>Jamy</u>'s words are spelt weirdly to show you <u>how</u> to say them with the right <u>Scottish accent</u>. He uses lots of words like '<u>sall</u>' (shall), '<u>baith</u>' (both), '<u>vary</u>' (very) etc.

<u>Macmorris</u> says things like '<u>ish</u>' (is), '<u>tish</u>' (it is/'tis) — he says '<u>s</u>' as '<u>sh</u>'.

Changing water language — dye-a-lake...

Blimey — this play's <u>full</u> of different languages. <u>Don't worry</u> about all the French — you can <u>work it out</u> even if you <u>don't</u> speak the lingo. Watch out for the key features of <u>Llewellyn</u>, <u>Jamy</u> and <u>Macmorris</u>' language too. You could get a scene with <u>Llewellyn</u> in, so be sure you <u>understand</u> him.

Images In The Play

This play's full of <u>images</u> — some people say they're there to make the language <u>rich</u> and <u>interesting</u>. I reckon they just make it a lot <u>trickier to follow</u>, myself.

Learn *these* Four Kinds *of* Image *to* Look Out For

Images are just <u>word pictures</u> — they help you see what Shakespeare's describing.
You'll pick up <u>loads</u> of marks for <u>spotting</u> them in your SAT scene, <u>and</u> giving them the <u>right name</u>.

① <u>Similes</u> are when one thing is <u>like</u> something else.

> The hedges <u>look like</u> wild-haired prisoners.

> as fluent as the sea
> Act 3, Scene 8, 31

> Her hedges, even-pleachèd.
> Like prisoners wildly overgrown with hair
> Put forth disordered twigs.
> Act 5, Scene 2, 42-4

They're a kind of <u>comparison</u> — and Shakespeare sticks them in all over the place.

② A <u>metaphor</u> is when he says one thing <u>is</u> something else.
Usually it just means using <u>exaggerated language</u> to <u>describe</u> things.

♫ ...How much is that doggy in the window — the one with the wagg-er-ly tail?...

> The earth sings when he touches it.
> Act 3, Scene 8, 15-16

The earth <u>can't</u> really sing — it's an image.

> When creeping murmur and the poring dark
> Fills the wide vessel of the universe.
> Act 4, Chorus, 2-3

The universe <u>isn't</u> really a wide vessel.

③ <u>Personification</u> means describing a thing <u>as if</u> it were a <u>person</u>.

> Upon the valleys, whose low vassal seat
> The Alps doth spit and void his rheum upon.
> Act 3, Scene 6, 51-2

He describes the Alps <u>spitting up a big greenie</u> on the valleys.

> And the third hour of drowsy morning name,
> Act 4, Chorus, 16

'Drowsy' makes you feel how <u>early</u> it is in the morning.

④ <u>Epic similes</u> are <u>longer comparisons</u>, made up of a <u>series</u> of <u>similes</u> that all <u>go together</u>.
They're often <u>based</u> on things from <u>ancient history</u>, such as Greek or Roman events.

Here <u>King Henry's arrival</u> in London is compared to the Roman general <u>Julius Caesar's triumphant arrival</u> back in Rome.

> The mayor and all his brethren in best sort,
> Like to the senators of th'antique Rome,
> With the plebeians swarming at their heels,
> Go forth and fetch their conquering Caesar in —
> Act 5, Chorus, 25-8

A spitting hotel — I'd like a rheum with a view...

Learn the <u>four kinds</u> of <u>image</u> now, and <u>practise</u> spotting them in the <u>play's key scenes</u> (section 9).

Common Images

Now you know the <u>kind</u> of images to look out for, you've got to <u>learn</u> about the <u>common</u> images. These are the images that <u>keep turning up</u> in different bits of the play.

There are Loads of Nature Images

<u>Nature</u> images are used for <u>all sorts</u> of things in the play.

1) They're used for images of the <u>social order</u>. This <u>bee image</u> goes on for 17 lines in Act 1.

> For so work the honey bees,
> Creatures that by a rule in nature teach
> The act of order to a peopled kingdom.
> Act 1, Scene 2, 187-189

2) The <u>English soldiers</u> are often compared to <u>dogs</u> — sometimes as an <u>insult</u>, sometimes as a <u>heroic</u> image.

> I see you stand like greyhounds in the slips,
> Act 3, Scene 1, 31

King Henry compares his soldiers to greyhounds <u>straining</u> at the leash.

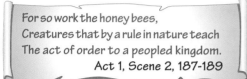

Are you calling me stupid?

> And the men do sympathise with the mastiffs in robustuous and rough coming on, leaving their wits with their wives.
> Act 3, Scene 8, 130-2

The French compare the English to a <u>brave</u> but quite <u>stupid</u> type of dog, a <u>mastiff</u>. In Shakespeare's time they were used in <u>dogfights</u> where they would attack <u>bears</u> and <u>bulls</u>.

3) There are lots of images of <u>flowers</u> and <u>plants</u>.

> As gardeners do with ordure hide those roots
> That shall first spring and be most delicate.
> Act 2, Scene 4, 39-40

The French Constable describes how Henry <u>hid</u> his heroic side when he was <u>younger</u>. He uses an image of <u>manure</u> hiding a flower. He's saying <u>appearances aren't</u> what they <u>seem</u>.

4) The play has lots of <u>storm</u> and <u>sea</u> images — this one's about a whirlpool.

> Therefore in fierce tempest is he coming,
> In thunder and in earthquake, like a Jove,
> Act 2, Scene 4, 100-101

> For England his approaches makes as fierce
> As waters to the sucking of a gulf.
> Act 2, Scene 4, 9-10

Watch Out for Ancient History Images too

The play's chock full of images from <u>ancient history</u>, especially <u>Llewellyn's</u> speeches. He talks about <u>famous generals</u> like Caesar, Pompey and <u>Alexander the 'Pig'</u>(Great) who he <u>compares</u> to <u>King Henry</u>.

> As Alexander killed his friend Cleitus, being in his ales and his cups, so also Harry Monmouth, being in his right wits and good judgements, turned away the fat knight with the great belly doublet.
> Act 4, Scene 7, 41-5

Alexander the pig — what a boaring image...

<u>Henry V</u> is stuffed full of imagery. Make sure you know <u>what</u> to <u>look out</u> for — <u>nature</u> and <u>history</u>.

Revision Summary

Flamin' Nora — this language lark is no picnic. Make sure you've been through this section carefully. It'll help you to spot the different tricks Shakespeare uses in some scenes. But before that, it'll help you answer these revision questions. I know they're a pain, but they're the only way you can test what you know. Have a go at them right now. If you get stuck with any, then go back and look over the section again. Then have another go. You should be getting the whole lot absolutely right before you're finished.

1) Is the best way to work out the language to read it out loud or to kidnap some actors?

2) What does every line of poetry start with?   a) 'Thou'   b) a capital letter   c) a comma.

3) What is prose?   a) normal writing that isn't poetry   b) the fronts of several boats.

4) What does it mean when King Henry calls himself 'we'?   And when he calls himself 'I'?

5) What do 'thou' and 'thee' mean?   What does 'thy' mean?

6) How many syllables does every line of poetry have?   a) 9   b) 10   c) 10 or 11.

7) What does Shakespeare sometimes do to make words fit the line?   a) change the word order   b) write nonsense   c) write with a quill pen   d) leave words out.
(there are two correct answers here — see if you can get both)

8) Should you stop reading at the end of each line of poetry?

9) What is blank verse?   a) poetry you can't understand   b) poetry that doesn't rhyme   c) poetry with words missing   d) poetry in French.

10) What kind of language are the Chorus' speeches in?   a) poetry   b) prose   c) Welsh.

11) When does Shakespeare use poetry in the play?

12) When does he use prose in the play?   a) at the end   b) when he's bored   c) the funny bits.

13) Give two types of speechmaking trick used in *Henry V*.   a) alliteration and line-dancing   b) rhetorical questions and exaggeration   c) magic threes and cracking fours.

14) Name two characters who speak difficult language in the play.

15) Name four kinds of image to look out for?
a) similes, metaphors, eric's similes and thingumajigs   b) similes, Betty Ford, personification and epic similes   c) similes, metaphors, personification and epic similes.

16) Name three nature images in the play.   a) flowers, storms and pussy cats   b) flowers, storms and dogs   c) flowers, hippies and peace, man.

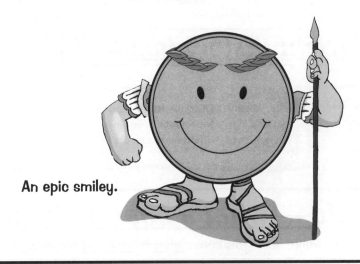

An epic smiley.

King Henry

King Henry is the most <u>important</u> character in the play — that's why it's called <u>*Henry V*</u> after all. Unfortunately, he's a bit of a slippery customer. There are definitely <u>two sides</u> to him.

King Henry *is a* <u>Tricky Character</u> *to Work Out*

1) Some bits of the play make him out to be a <u>hero</u>. He gives <u>inspiring speeches</u> to fire his men up. He's a very good <u>soldier</u> — he <u>wins</u> at Agincourt against a much <u>bigger army</u>.

2) He can also be quite <u>ruthless and cruel</u> — he makes lots of <u>vicious threats</u> at the siege of Harfleur, and at one point he even orders his men to <u>kill</u> all their prisoners.

3) He has a few <u>human moments</u>, too. He goes around the camp in disguise to talk to his men, but ends up <u>arguing</u> with one of his soldiers. He has a key speech in <u>Act 4, Scene 1</u>, where he talks about the <u>difficulties</u> of <u>being king</u>, and being <u>blamed</u> for everything that goes wrong.

> <u>Look out</u> for these things in what King Henry <u>says</u> and <u>does</u> in the <u>scene</u> you get in the Exam.

He <u>Used</u> *to be a Real* <u>Tearaway</u>

In <u>Act 1, Scene 1</u>, the two bishops talk about what a rebel he used to be, and how he's really <u>changed</u>:

> The King is full of grace and holy regard.
> Act 1, Scene 1, 22

Some of the French think he's <u>still</u> a waster and underestimate how good a leader he is:

> Her sceptre so fantastically borne,
> By a vain, giddy, shallow, humorous youth,
> Act 2, Scene 4, 27-8

Some *People Say Henry's a* Strong Leader

Aww... kittens...

purrrrrrrrrrrr...

King Henry was a strong leader — except when it came to cats.

1) In <u>Act 1, Scene 2</u>, some people say that Henry shows he is in <u>complete control</u>. He decides to invade France and makes sure <u>everyone</u> is behind him. He answers the Dauphin's tennis ball insult <u>without</u> being immature or petty.

2) His battle speeches seem to show he <u>respects</u> his men and <u>trusts</u> them to fight well. He <u>isn't afraid</u> to <u>die</u> himself, since he <u>refuses</u> to agree a <u>ransom</u> with the French. Henry talks about <u>equality</u> between him and his men in battle — he says they're all <u>brothers</u>.

> We few, we happy few, we band of brothers;
> For he today that sheds his blood with me
> Shall be my brother.
> Act 4, Scene 3, 60-62

3) He actually talks to <u>ordinary soldiers</u> — especially <u>Llewellyn</u> after the battle, in <u>Act 4, Scene 7</u>. He even goes around the camp in <u>disguise</u> before Agincourt, so he can talk to his men. The French nobles <u>never</u> speak to ordinary soldiers — this shows Henry is a <u>better leader</u>.

King Henry

Wait for it — there's a lot <u>more</u> to Henry than <u>just</u> being a strong king.

Some People Say Henry's Cruel and Only Wants Glory

1) Right from <u>Act 1</u>, it's clear Henry's very <u>ambitious</u>. He <u>doesn't care</u> who gets in his way. He threatens to <u>take money</u> from the Church in Act 1 — they end up offering to <u>pay</u> for his war.

Don't stand in my way!

2) In <u>Act 2</u>, he <u>threatens</u> the French King with a <u>horrible war</u>, and has the <u>three traitors</u> Scroop, Gray and Cambridge <u>executed</u> for their treason.

3) In <u>Act 2, Scene 1</u>, we find out that Henry used to be <u>best mates</u> with <u>Sir John Falstaff</u>, but then <u>rejected</u> him when he became King. In <u>Act 2, Scene 3</u>, we find out that Falstaff has <u>died</u> of a <u>broken heart</u>.

4) In Act 3, Henry tries to <u>inspire</u> his men but <u>none</u> of them are interested — they're <u>fighting</u> among themselves (Act 3, Scenes 2-3). Henry's speech to the Governor of Harfleur is full of <u>violent threats</u> (Act 3, Scene 4).

5) When he hears his old friend Bardolph is going to be <u>hanged</u> for stealing, he doesn't save him — he appears <u>ruthless</u> and <u>determined</u> here, as if he never knew Bardolph.

6) During the battle, Henry <u>orders</u> his soldiers to <u>kill</u> the French prisoners. This is <u>against</u> all the <u>rules of war</u> because all the prisoners had <u>surrendered</u>, so they <u>should</u> have been protected.

He Enjoys Playing Tricks on People

In <u>Act 2, Scene 2</u>, Henry traps the <u>traitors</u> by telling them about a man who <u>insulted</u> him. The traitors say he should <u>punish</u> the man. When <u>their plot</u> is revealed Henry tells them <u>they</u> will be given the <u>same mercy</u> they showed to the other man — <u>none</u>.

SNICKER... CHORTLE...

Ace Whoopee Cushion

He puts on <u>disguise</u> to visit his soldiers in <u>Act 4, Scene 1</u>. He tries to encourage them but finds himself arguing with Bates, Court and Williams. He and Williams argue about whether the King is <u>right</u> to have brought so many men into battle where they might die. Henry loses his temper and ends up challenging Williams to a <u>duel</u> after the battle.

In Act 4, Scenes 7-8, he plays a trick on <u>Llewellyn</u> and <u>Williams</u>. <u>Williams</u> has Henry's glove — Henry tells <u>Llewellyn</u> there's a <u>traitor</u> wearing that glove. It very nearly causes a <u>major fight</u>, but Henry <u>steps in</u> and explains who he really is to Williams. Williams pleads for his life — Henry <u>lets him off</u> and <u>rewards</u> him for his courage.

Henry has Some Doubts and Fears

In Act 4, Scene 1, Henry worries about the <u>pressures</u> of being King — he thinks his subjects have an <u>easier life</u> than he does. He also feels <u>guilty</u> because his father <u>took over</u> as King by forcing Richard II to <u>give up</u> his power. He prays to God and asks <u>not</u> to be <u>punished</u> for <u>his father's sin</u>. He says he's done his best to <u>make up</u> for it — he reburied Richard II and dedicated 2 chapels to him.

In the play, Henry is sometimes called '<u>The King</u>', sometimes '<u>King Henry</u>', and sometimes '<u>Harry</u>' or '<u>King Harry</u>'. In this book, we've usually called him <u>Henry</u> or <u>King Henry</u>.

Henry V — I hate these sequels...

You'll <u>almost definitely</u> get a task about Henry, so be sure to <u>learn</u> everything on these two pages.

English Nobles

OK, these fellas <u>aren't</u> exactly thrilling, but they could easily <u>turn up</u> in your SAT scene. You've got to know <u>who</u> they all are, just in case — or you could find yourself in <u>big trouble</u>.

Exeter is Henry's Uncle

He's <u>wise</u> and very <u>brave</u>. King Henry sends him to France as an <u>ambassador</u> in <u>Act 2, Scene 4</u>, and he's dead rude to the Dauphin — he demands that the French pay a <u>high price</u> to stop Henry invading. He's <u>brave</u> in defending the <u>bridge</u>, as reported by Llewellyn in <u>Act 3, Scene 7</u>.

Three lions on a shirt...

Gloucester, Bedford and Clarence — Henry's brothers

These three really <u>aren't</u> very exciting. They appear in the <u>Court</u> scenes in England, before the <u>battle of Agincourt</u> and in the <u>peace negotiations</u> and that's it.

Don't Forget all the Other Ones...

<u>Westmorland</u> wishes for <u>more troops</u> before the Battle of Agincourt — but he's definitely a <u>brave</u> and <u>respected</u> soldier.

<u>Erpingham</u> is an <u>old knight</u> with plenty of fighting experience — the King and the army all <u>respect</u> him.

Good job we got these name tags, eh?

Erpingham

Warwick

Westmorland

Salisbury

York

<u>Warwick</u> is at the battle — he's mentioned in <u>Act 4, Scenes 7-8</u>. Henry asks him to make sure the fight between <u>Williams</u> and <u>Llewellyn</u> doesn't get too serious.

<u>Salisbury</u> is another English noble who appears in the battle scenes. Exeter and Bedford say how <u>brave</u> he is.

<u>York</u> leads the vanguard (front line) of the English army, and gets <u>killed</u> in the battle. Exeter describes his heroic death in <u>Act 4, Scene 6, 7-32</u>.

The English lords didn't ring — no-bells, you see...

Remember, Exeter is quite a bit <u>older</u> than King Henry. He's wise and experienced, and gets stuck in to the battles <u>and</u> the politics. <u>All</u> the English nobles are supposed to be <u>really brave</u>.

Bishops & Traitors

The bishops and the traitors both appear quite early on in the play. You learn about what King Henry's like by the way he talks to them, and how he reacts to what they do.

Canterbury and Ely are Clever Politicians

Canterbury's an Archbishop — he's the head of the Church in England.
Ely is a Bishop — a less powerful figure.

Are you a Bish, too?

No, I'm an actor.

1) They discuss how King Henry has changed from a lazy rebel to an ideal king in Act 1, Scene 1. They're also worried because King Henry wants to take land and money away from the Church.

2) They suggest a war with France and offer to pay for it, so Henry can win glory.

3) Canterbury makes a huge and really boring speech about French law in Act 1, Scene 2. It's there to explain how Henry can claim to be the rightful King of France.

4) Henry likes the idea because it allows him to be a hero without having to shell out for an expensive war.

Scroop, Cambridge and Gray are English Traitors

These three rogues only appear in Act 2, Scene 2. We find out straightaway from Bedford, Exeter and Westmorland that they're traitors. King Henry pretends he still trusts them to run the kingdom when he's away. He then gives them pieces of paper charging them with treason:

Uh-oh...

Read them, and know I know your worthiness.
Act 2, Scene 2, 67

Henry tricks them. He's already made them say that they think anyone who does something against the King should be executed, then he reveals that he knows they're traitors. They can't ask for mercy now, so they're sentenced to death.

When they are arrested, all three of them make confessions, admitting what they've done. In some productions of the play, they are tortured to force them to confess like this. In other productions they do it to beg for forgiveness. All three are taken away to be executed.

These Bishops — they're Ely politicians...

The boring bits with the two bishops tell you a lot about why King Henry decides to start the war. The traitors are really there to show you what Henry's like — firm but fair. Remember who's who.

Llewellyn & Pistol

These two may not be the funniest guys in the world, but they are the funniest characters in the play. They're amusing mainly because of the way they talk.

Llewellyn is a Brave but Funny Character

1) Llewellyn is a professional captain in Henry's army. He's Welsh. In some versions of the play, he's called Fluellen — that's the way Shakespeare would have pronounced the Welsh name Llewellyn.

Don't call me Taffy...

2) He's used for humour in the play, especially because of his Welsh accent. He pronounces 'b' as 'p' and uses lots of fancy words.

3) He knows a lot about wars from history, and he's proud of it. At the siege of Harfleur, he wants a debate with the Irish captain Macmorris about tactics. It's funny because Llewellyn is so over the top:

> Captain Macmorris, I beseech you now, will you vouchsafe me, look you, a few disputations with you as partly touching or concerning the disciplines of the wars, the Roman wars, in the way of argument, look you, and friendly communication?
>
> Act 3, Scene 3, 36-40

4) Henry plays a trick on him and Williams in Act 4, Scenes 7-8.

5) Llewellyn is brave and very principled. He's a real soldier and he hates cowards. Pistol mocks Llewellyn for being Welsh. He gets his own back by forcing Pistol to eat a leek.

> By Cheshu, I will make him eat some part of my leek, or I will peat his pate four days. Bite, I pray you, it is good for your green wound and your ploody coxcomb.
>
> Act 5, Scene 1, 36-38

Pistol is a Coward and a Boaster

1) Pistol is one of Henry's ex-drinking companions — a mate of Sir John Falstaff's. After Falstaff dies, he goes to the war to make money out of it.

2) Pistol speaks in a funny overblown sort of way, with lots of fancy words and alliteration. It's a joke version of old fashioned heroic speech (see Section 4).

3) He's a coward, and a bit of a conman. Gower says Pistol pretends to have been at all the battles so people will think he's a great soldier.

4) He takes a French prisoner in Act 4, Scene 4 and hopes to get some money from him, but he has to kill him to follow Henry's orders.

5) By the end of the play, Pistol has been forced to eat a leek by Llewellyn as punishment for insulting him. All his friends are dead, so he decides to return to London to be a thief and a pimp.

Just like Noel — he's a right Coward...

Pistol and Llewellyn are both comedy characters in the play, but they're very different people. Llewellyn takes the war really seriously and wants to do well. Pistol's just a freeloading coward.

Bardolph, Nym & Boy

Bardolph, Nym and the Boy are <u>Pistol's mates</u>. You probably won't get asked about one of them <u>on his own</u>, but you could well be asked about <u>all four together</u>.

Bardolph *is a* Drunk *and a* Thief

<u>Bardolph</u> is another of Henry's <u>ex-drinking pals</u> —
he hangs around with Pistol and Nym. He's a terrible
drunkard. Llewellyn describes his <u>red nose</u> and <u>spots</u>.

He's a <u>thief</u>, as well. The <u>Boy</u> says he and Nym are both thieves.
By <u>Act 3, Scene 7</u>, he's sentenced to be <u>hanged</u> for stealing
from a <u>church</u>. Llewellyn tells King Henry, who <u>ignores</u> the fact
that he once <u>knew</u> Bardolph.

Nym *is a Low-Life* Too

If it ain't nailed
down, I'll have it.

<u>Nym</u> goes around with Pistol and Bardolph, and he is just as much
of a <u>thieving loser</u>. We're told he's been <u>hanged</u> in <u>Act 4, Scene 4</u>.

In Act 1, Scene 2 he gets into a fight with <u>Pistol</u> because
Pistol's <u>married</u> the girl he thought <u>he</u> was <u>engaged</u> to.

Nym goes to France, but he'd rather <u>not</u> be involved in any
actual <u>fighting</u>. The Boy says he's a <u>thief</u> and a <u>coward</u>.

Nym and Bardolph are sworn brothers in filching...
Act 3, Scene 2, 39-40

The Boy *is a Servant*

The Boy used to be <u>Falstaff's servant</u>, but when Falstaff dies he goes to
France as a servant to Pistol, Nym and Bardolph. He has to look after
the <u>luggage</u> in the English camp when the soldiers are off fighting.

He's a very <u>good judge of character</u>. He describes <u>exactly</u> what
Pistol, Bardolph and Nym are like. He wants to <u>leave</u> them as soon
as possible, because he knows they're no good (Act 3, Scene 2).

He speaks <u>French</u>, so he <u>interprets</u> in the comic
scene with Pistol's prisoner — at the end he says:

So, why do
they just call
you "Boy"?

Well, I did have
a name, but I've
forgotten it...

The French might have a good prey of us, if he knew of
it, for there is none to guard it but boys.
Act 4, Scene 4, 59-61

He ends up being <u>killed</u>
by the French when they
<u>attack</u> the <u>English camp</u>.

A talented pickpocket — Nym-ble fingered...

The <u>Boy</u> is an important character because he <u>tells you</u> what the <u>other characters</u> are like. <u>Nym</u> and
<u>Bardolph</u> are as bad as each <u>other</u>. Remember, Bardolph's the <u>drunk</u> and Nym's the <u>coward</u>.

The English Army

Crumbs, even <u>more</u> characters — some of the <u>soldiers</u> from the English army. Bates, Court and Williams are <u>key characters</u> because of the <u>discussion</u> they have with <u>Henry</u>.

Gower, Macmorris and Jamy are Army Captains

<u>Gower</u> is an honest, well-respected <u>English captain</u>.

Come on, chaps, let's be sensible...

Gower tries to keep the peace betwen <u>Llewellyn</u> and <u>Macmorris</u> in <u>Act 3, Scene 3</u>. In <u>Act 3, Scene 7</u>, he puts Llewellyn right when Llewellyn <u>doesn't realise</u> that Pistol is a <u>liar</u>.

After Llewellyn makes Pistol eat a leek in <u>Act 5, Scene 1</u>, Gower gives Pistol a serious <u>telling off</u> for misjudging Llewellyn because he's Welsh.

> You thought because he could not speak English in the native garb, he could not therefore handle an English cudgel. You find it otherwise, and henceforth let a Welsh correction teach you a good English condition.
> Act 5, Scene 1, 66-70

<u>Jamy</u> is <u>Scottish</u> and <u>Macmorris</u> is <u>Irish</u>.

They only appear in <u>Act 3, Scene 3</u>. Both of them speak 'comedy' versions of Irish and Scottish accents.

Macmorris flies right off the handle when he thinks Llewellyn is <u>insulting</u> his <u>Irishness</u>.

Bates, Court and Williams are Ordinary Soldiers

These lads are just three <u>ordinary soldiers</u>. King Henry meets them when he goes through the camp in disguise in <u>Act 4, Scene 1</u>.

> I beseech you take it for your own fault and not mine, for had you been as I took you for, I made no offence...
> Act 4, Scene 8, 49-51

1) They have a <u>bitter</u> conversation where they <u>argue</u> about the King's <u>responsibility</u> for the situation. They're <u>ordinary soldiers</u> who are <u>worried</u> about <u>dying</u> in the battle. They <u>blame</u> the King for the <u>desperate</u> situation.

2) Henry says it isn't the King's fault at all, and ends up <u>quarrelling</u> with Williams. Williams <u>challenges</u> him to a <u>duel</u>.

3) After the battle Henry plays a <u>trick</u> on Williams. Then, Henry reveals that <u>he</u> was the man Williams had <u>challenged</u>. Williams' challenge is a form of <u>treason</u>.

4) Williams <u>stands up</u> for himself — he says the King <u>can't expect</u> people to treat him like a King if he goes round in <u>disguise</u>. Henry takes that as a fair point, pardons Williams and gives him his glove filled with gold coins as a <u>reward</u>.

Cap'n Mac-morris — the hat and raincoat dance...

Imagine finding out you'd nearly got into a <u>scrap</u> with your own <u>King</u> — what a mistake to make. Luckily King Henry <u>admires</u> the way Williams stands up for himself, so <u>no harm's done</u>.

The French Royal Family

The <u>French King</u> appears in a <u>couple</u> of scenes, and so does his daughter <u>Katherine</u>.

The French King is Cautious

1) The French King <u>doesn't rush</u> into things. When Exeter tells him that Henry plans to take the French throne, the French King <u>doesn't</u> give an <u>immediate answer</u> — he'd rather <u>sleep</u> on it.

2) He offers his <u>daughter</u> to Henry — if they marry, the peace between France and England ought to <u>last</u>.

3) In <u>Act 5, Scene 2</u>, he <u>isn't ready</u> to give an answer right away, either. He asks to look through the peace treaty <u>again</u> before he signs up to it.

4) The <u>real</u> French King was <u>mad</u>, but the character in the play <u>isn't</u>.

5) The French Queen is barely in the play at <u>all</u>. She comes in at the end, where she's glad that France and England <u>aren't</u> <u>fighting</u> any more. She wants the peace deal to work out OK.

Katherine is the French King's daughter

You see Katherine <u>twice</u> in the play — once when she's <u>learning English</u>, and once when Henry <u>speaks to</u> her.

In <u>Act 3, Scene 5</u>, Katherine asks her lady in waiting, <u>Alice</u>, to teach her <u>English</u>. It's quite a <u>funny</u> scene because of the way Katherine pronounces the English words in a ridiculous French way.

She's learning English because she already knows she'll have to <u>marry Henry</u> as part of a <u>peace deal</u>. In those days, princes and princesses usually had <u>arranged marriages</u> for political reasons.

In the <u>final scene</u> Henry <u>chats her up</u> and tries to make her like him. She says she'll only consent if Henry will love <u>France</u>, too. Remember, Katherine <u>doesn't</u> really have a <u>choice</u> — the scene just makes it <u>seem</u> like she does.

The Dauphin is the French King's son

<u>Dauphin</u> is the <u>title</u> of the <u>eldest son</u> of the French King. It's a similar idea to calling the Queen of England's eldest son 'Prince of Wales'. His coat of arms is a <u>dolphin</u> — 'dauphin' is French for dolphin.

The Dauphin is cocky and <u>arrogant</u> — he sends <u>tennis balls</u> to Henry as a joke. He <u>isn't afraid</u> of Henry, but ends up being <u>proved wrong</u>.

The French King <u>refuses</u> to let him go to battle. In some versions of the play, the Dauphin <u>does</u> turn up to the battle and speaks Bourbon's lines in <u>Act 3, Scene 8</u>, and <u>Act 4, Scenes 2 and 5</u>.

A dolphin prince — what's the porpoise...

These <u>French royals</u> don't have an awful lot of lines, especially <u>Katherine</u>. What <u>King Henry</u> says to <u>her</u> is <u>more important</u> than what <u>she</u> says to <u>him</u>. Watch out for the <u>Dauphin's criticisms</u> of Henry.

The Constable, Orléans & Bourbon

The French nobles are all a bit <u>ridiculous</u>. They're more concerned with <u>posing</u> than winning a war.

The <u>Constable</u> is in Charge of the <u>Army</u>

OK, it's <u>obvious</u>, but don't forget it — the Constable <u>isn't</u> a policeman. It's his <u>title</u>.
It means he's head of the royal household and <u>commander</u> of the <u>army</u>.

> Ooh, what a lovely war.

In Act 2, Scene 4, he's the <u>voice of reason</u>. He knows Henry's a good leader and that the French <u>ought</u> to be <u>worried</u>.

Before the battle he goes on about how <u>posh</u> his <u>armour</u> is, and then gets involved in a general discussion about <u>horses</u> and <u>mistresses</u>.
He ends up <u>arguing</u> with <u>Bourbon</u> — showing how <u>divided</u> the French are.

The Constable is <u>over-confident</u> — he thinks the French will win easily.
It <u>doesn't</u> work out well for him though — he's the <u>first name</u> on the list of <u>dead</u> French nobles in <u>Act 4, Scene 8</u>.

Orléans is the French King's Nephew

Orléans takes part in the <u>discussion</u> before the battle in <u>Act 3, Scene 8</u>.
He <u>starts</u> the argument about who has the <u>best horse</u>.

When the French realise they're losing, Orléans points out that they could <u>still win</u> if they <u>reorganised</u> themselves.

He's captured and kept <u>prisoner</u> at the end of the battle.

Bourbon is Arrogant but Daft

Bourbon is <u>arrogant</u>, but not quite on the ball.
He's meant to be a silly character.

Before the battle in <u>Act 3, Scene 8</u> he makes loads of <u>ridiculous</u> boasts about his <u>horse</u>. The Constable <u>takes the mickey</u> out of him.

When the French start losing, he <u>panics</u>. He says everyone should <u>stab themselves</u>, which would be pointless. Then he decides to go back and <u>fight</u> so he can die bravely.
He <u>doesn't listen</u> when Orléans says they should try <u>reorganising</u> their forces.

> The devil take order now, I'll to the throng.
> Let life be short, else shame will be too long.
> Act 4, Scene 5, 23-24

In <u>Act 4, Scene 7</u> Bourbon is brought on as a <u>prisoner</u> by the English army.

Bourbon's boasts — they take the biscuit...

These <u>French nobles</u> are quite a bit different from the English nobles. Their attitudes are certainly different — they're so <u>over-confident</u> and boastful that they're <u>bound</u> to be heading for a <u>fall</u>.

Other French Nobles & Burgundy

Burgundy has a couple of important speeches in Act 5, Scene 2. The other French nobles don't say much. They're there to make up numbers, so the French court looks more impressive.

Here are a few Other French Nobles

Lots of other French nobles pop up from time to time, but you don't need to know much about them. Basically, they're all confident of a French victory, and stunned at the defeat.

Shame we're not in it much...

Britain

Berri

Grandpré

Bof...

Rambures

Grandpré speaks before the battle to encourage the French nobles and mock the English.

Britain is the Duke of Brittany, not Britain. He doesn't say anything at all.

Berri doesn't say anything either.

Rambures joins in with a few of the conversations.

A lot of these names come from the list of dead nobles given in the history books that Shakespeare used to get his facts about the battle.

Burgundy is the Go-Between in the Peace Talks

Burgundy is the ruler of an independent area which is neutral — not completely under French or English control.

Ooh, suits you, sir!

He appears in Act 5, Scene 2, to help sort out the peace treaty. He makes a long sad speech about how France has been left to rot.

> And as our vineyards, fallows, meads and hedges
> Defective in their nature grow to wildness...
> Act 5, Scene 2, 54-5

When the treaty's all sorted out he comes back in and makes lots of jokes about sex to King Henry. It's all very silly, and out of place:

> Can you blame her, then, being a maid rosed over with the virgin crimson of modesty, if she deny the appearance of a naked blind boy in her naked seeing self? 'Tis a hard condition for a maid to consign to.
> Act 5, Scene 2, 266-69

Who are these guys — Burgundy if I know...

Right then — the one thing you need to remember here is that in the play, Burgundy is a neutral figure. He appears in Act 5, Scene 2 as a go-between to help work out the peace treaty.

Montjoy & Chorus

Now these two are <u>dead important</u> in the play — especially the <u>Chorus</u>.

Montjoy *is the* French Herald

His job is to carry <u>messages</u> between the two armies — first from the King of France to Henry, then from Constable to Henry. Montjoy is really his <u>title</u>, <u>not</u> his name.

At first his attitude to King Henry is <u>rude</u>.
He <u>doesn't</u> even address him as a king:

> You know me by my habit.
> Act 3, Scene 7, 105

<u>Habit</u> means the <u>clothes</u> he wears as <u>herald</u>.

As time goes on, Montjoy shows Henry <u>more respect</u>. The second time he's sent, he calls Henry 'King Harry'. Henry replies <u>defiantly</u>, but very <u>politely</u>:

> Herald, save thou thy labour,
> Come thou no more for ransom, gentle herald...
> Act 4, Scene 3, 121-22

The word '<u>thou</u>' instead of 'you' could be <u>rude</u> or <u>friendly</u> (see Section 4).

In <u>Act 4, Scene 7</u>, Montjoy comes back. He tells Henry that the <u>English</u> have <u>won</u>, and asks <u>permission</u> to bury the French dead. Gloucester says Montjoy's eyes are "humbler".

The Chorus *is the* Narrator

The Chorus is the <u>first person</u> we see on stage. He tells us the <u>story</u>, <u>describes</u> things and fills us in on bits that the play has <u>missed out</u>.

He recognises that this play is really <u>too big</u> for the stage — you can't have life-sized battles with <u>cannons</u> and <u>horses</u> in a <u>theatre</u>. He says the stage can't do it justice, so the audience will have to use their <u>imaginations</u>.

> Piece out our imperfections with your thoughts.
> Prologue, 23

We've used this bloke for our Chorus.

At beginning of each act, the Chorus tells the audience <u>where</u> the action has moved to and <u>sets the scene</u>.

The Chorus speaks in very <u>beautiful</u> <u>poetry</u>, especially in Acts 4 and 5.

<u>Different productions</u> show the Chorus in lots of different ways. Sometimes the Chorus is played in <u>modern clothes</u>, sometimes as <u>Britannia</u>, sometimes as a personification of <u>History</u>. It's all up to the <u>director</u> at the end of the day.

French messages — les cartes postales...

It's Montjoy's <u>job</u> to carry messages between the two sides — <u>King Henry</u> actually <u>pays</u> him for it. The <u>Chorus</u> comments on all the action of the play, and tells us what's going to <u>happen</u>.

Minor Characters

These bods are worth <u>storing</u> in your memory <u>just in case</u> they show up in your SAT scene.

The <u>Governor of Harfleur</u> Surrenders

He had asked the <u>Dauphin</u> for help, but the French army <u>weren't ready</u> to come and defend the town.

Once the English have surrounded the town, the people of Harfleur will <u>starve</u> if they don't surrender, so in <u>Act 3, Scene 4</u>, the Governor gives in.

> Therefore, great King,
> We yield our town and lives to thy soft mercy.
> Act 3, Scene 4, 47-48

The <u>Hostess</u> is <u>Pistol's Wife</u>

She is <u>hostess</u>, or landlady, of a pub in London.

1) She was in *Henry IV*, and *The Merry Wives of Windsor*. In those plays she's called Mistress Quickly.

2) She was engaged to <u>Nym</u> for some time — and in <u>Act 2, Scene 1</u>, Nym is still rather <u>cross</u> that she ended up <u>marrying Pistol</u>.

3) She looks after <u>Falstaff</u> while he's dying, and <u>describes</u> his death in <u>Act 2, Scene 3</u>. After that she disappears from the play.

<u>Le Fer</u> is a <u>French Soldier</u> taken <u>Prisoner</u>

<u>Pistol</u> takes him <u>prisoner</u> in Act 4, Scene 4. Pistol demands a <u>big ransom</u>.

Le Fer is <u>terrified</u>. He tries to beg for his life. Unfortunately, Pistol <u>doesn't</u> speak <u>French</u>, so they have a <u>conversation</u> where they both fail to <u>understand</u> what the other is saying.

> FRENCH   Est-il impossible d'échapper la force de ton bras?
> PISTOL   Brass, cur? Thou damnèd and luxurious mountain goat, offer'st me brass?
> Act 4, Scene 4, 13-15

Finally the Boy comes along and <u>translates</u>, so you can follow what Le Fer says. He offers Pistol <u>a lot of money</u>, but then Henry orders the English to <u>kill</u> all their prisoners. Pistol is left with <u>nothing</u>.

<u>Thanks for sparing a life — pleading for merci...</u>

You <u>don't</u> need to know as much about these people as you do about the <u>main characters</u>. The key thing is to make sure you know <u>who</u> they are, just in case they get <u>mentioned</u> in your <u>SAT scene</u>.

Revision Summary

Blimey, talk about a lot of characters... The key to the play is understanding King Henry. He speaks about a third of the lines in the play. You need to know what kind of leader he is, and how he manages to keep his men's spirits up. Don't forget the rest of the characters though. Some of them aren't in it for all that long, but you need to know exactly who they are, and when their paths run across King Henry's in the play. It's all about knowing who's who.

1) Is King Henry: *a) strong but kind   b) ruthless and ambitious   or   c) both?*

2) What does Henry ask his soldiers to do that's against the rules of war?

3) What does King Henry do to keep his men's spirits up?

4) Who does Henry visit while he's in disguise?

5) What happens when King Henry talks to his soldiers before the Battle of Agincourt? Does he: *a) put the kettle on for a brew   b) tell them to fight bravely for England   c) sing some football songs at the top of his voice?*

6) What relation is Exeter to King Henry?

7) Which noble wishes for more troops before the Battle of Agincourt?

8) Who suggests the idea of a war with France to King Henry?

9) What are the names of the three traitors?

10) What does Llewellyn make Pistol eat?

11) Is Pistol really a good soldier, or is he just pretending?

12) Which character is the worst drunkard?

13) Is Pistol a lily-livered coward?

14) What is the Boy's job?

15) Which of the army captains gets annoyed with Llewellyn?

16) Are Bates, Court and Williams ordinary soldiers, or are they officers?

17) Whose daughter is Katherine?

18) What does Alice teach her?

19) Do the Constable, Orléans and Bourbon argue about: *a) who has the best horse   b) who has the most money   c) who makes the best chilli con carne?*

20) Is he called Constable because he's a policeman?

21) Who panics most when the French start losing?

22) Who helps sort out the peace treaty?

23) Who is the French Herald?

24) Who tells the audience what's going on?

25) Who is the Hostess married to?

26) What's the name of the French soldier taken prisoner by Pistol?

ACT 1 PROLOGUE, SCENE 1	# What Happens in Act One

In the test you <u>only</u> write about one scene, but that <u>doesn't</u> mean you can ignore the rest of the play. Use this section to get a handle on the <u>whole story</u>.

Prologue — The Chorus Sets the Scene

This story's too big for an ordinary theatre
The Chorus wishes there were real princes to act out the story, a whole kingdom as a theatre and kings and queens as an audience. Then it might be possible to give a good impression of King Henry and the war. The audience will have to use their imaginations to turn what they see into something as impressive as what actually happened. lines 1-34

Remember, this is based on <u>real history</u>. The Chorus is <u>apologising</u> that the play won't be as <u>exciting</u> as the real events, but he still makes you look forward to the play.

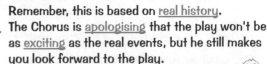

Scene One — The Bishops are Hoping for War

This first scene shows some <u>shady</u> behind-the-scenes political stuff.

The Archbishop of Canterbury is the head of the Church. He's the Bishop of Ely's <u>boss</u>.

They're not just talking about a few fields — Parliament wants to take away a lot of land. The <u>rent</u> people pay on it makes the Church pots of <u>money</u>.

The <u>French</u> know Henry's thinking about making war, and they've sent <u>ambassadors</u> to tell the English what they think.

1 **The Church is in trouble**
Canterbury tells Ely that a bill proposed in Parliament would take valuable lands away from the Church and give them to King Henry. lines 1-20

2 **Ely wants to know what can be done**
Ely asks how the Church can save the lands for itself. Canterbury doesn't answer straight away. He starts going on about Henry. lines 21-22

3 **Henry's turned over a new leaf**
Canterbury says Henry was a wild young man, but now he's king he's suddenly calm and wise. He spent his youth messing around, but now you would think he'd spent it all studying. lines 23-69

4 **Ely still wants to know about the bill**
He asks what Henry thinks about it. Canterbury says Henry seems likely to support the Church. Canterbury's offered Henry cash to help him fight a war for the French throne. lines 69-81

5 **Henry needs to be sure about making war**
Canterbury thinks Henry would have taken the cash if there'd been time to explain the claim to France more clearly. The French ambassadors have arrived and interrupted their conversation. lines 82-93

6 **It's time to talk to the French ambassadors**
Canterbury and Ely go to hear the French ambassadors deliver their message. lines 93-98

A meeting with Ely — fishy business...

<u>Brace yourself</u> — there's a heck of a pile of <u>learning</u> in this section. I'll admit the story <u>looks</u> pretty endless. Just take it <u>one scene at a time</u> and before you know it you'll have it <u>all covered</u>.

What Happens in Act One

I'll admit it — some scenes are definitely <u>more exciting</u> than others. That doesn't mean you can skip them though. You need to know the <u>whole story</u> to do well in your SAT.

Scene Two — Henry Decides on War with France

1   The English are waiting to see the Ambassadors
Henry wants to talk to Canterbury before the Ambassadors are called. lines 1-6

2   Canterbury and Ely arrive
Henry asks Canterbury to explain the Salic law. He wants to know if it prevents him claiming the French throne. Henry warns Canterbury not to twist the facts. lines 7-32

3   Canterbury explains the Salic law
The law says no woman can inherit in the 'Salic lands'. Canterbury says it doesn't apply. The Salic lands are in Germany, not France and many French kings have inherited the throne through their mothers. Canterbury tells Henry he is the true heir to the French throne. lines 33-95

Henry says he doesn't want to go to war if he can't <u>justify</u> it.

> For God doth know how many now in health
> Shall drop their blood in approbation
> Of what your reverence shall incite us to.
>   (18-20)

...he's <u>sharing the blame</u> with Canterbury.

Henry's claim to the French throne is through his <u>mother's side</u> of the family. That's why the French are trying to use this <u>Salic law</u> against him.

Canterbury compares Henry to his great-uncle <u>Edward</u>, who fought a <u>successful war</u> in France when he was Prince of Wales. He <u>won</u> the battle of Crécy against the French in 1346.

4   The bishops and nobles tell Henry to go for it
Canterbury, Ely, Exeter and Westmorland encourage Henry to go to war. Canterbury promises that the Church will support the war with money. lines 96-135

5   Henry's still not completely sure
Henry's worried the Scots will invade while he's away. The nobles agree that's more than likely, but say England can easily be defended against the Scots. lines 136-221

6   The French Ambassadors are called
While they're waiting for the Ambassadors, Henry announces that he's decided to go to war. He wants to go down in history. lines 222-233

7   The Ambassadors bring the Dauphin's message
The Dauphin dismisses Henry's claims. He has sent a deliberately insulting present of tennis balls. Henry tells the Ambassadors the Dauphin should have taken him more seriously. He warns that he will be declaring war. lines 234-298

8   Henry's mind is made up
He orders the nobles to start preparing troops and supplies. lines 299-310

The Dauphin's message — a load of balls...

Crikey, that <u>Canterbury</u> could talk the hind legs off a herd of zebras. <u>Don't worry</u> about the details of the Salic law — it's <u>meant</u> to be complicated. The main thing here is that Henry's <u>determined</u> to go to war, and the Dauphin's tennis-ball insult makes him <u>even more</u> determined.

ACT 2
CHORUS, SCENE 1

What Happens in Act Two

Act Two is where the <u>action</u> starts. Get to grips with the complete story now, and you'll find it <u>a squillion times easier</u> to write about the scene you get in the <u>test</u>.

Chorus — England gets Ready for War

> Now then, ladies and gents, we're off to Southampton to get the boat to France. Sit tight, and don't be seasick!

> Are we there yet?

1 **All England is busy preparing for the war**
Everyone is excited and preparing for the war. There are some people who are not so keen to help England though. The French have bribed Cambridge, Scroop and Gray to kill Henry before he sets sail for France. lines 1-30

2 **The action will be moving to Southampton**
The Chorus asks the audience to sit tight as the play takes them from London to Southampton, and on to France. lines 31-42

Scene One — Argey-bargey between Nym and Pistol

It's time to meet some real <u>lowlifes</u> — Nym, Bardolph, Pistol and the Hostess.

1 **Nym and Bardolph meet in the street**
Nym is furious with his friend Pistol. Pistol has got married to Nell Quickly. Nym thought Nell was going to marry him. lines 1-22

2 **Pistol and Nell arrive, Pistol and Nym quarrel**
Pistol and Nym draw their swords. They put them away when the Hostess asks them to, but the quarrel flares up again. Bardolph draws his sword and threatens them both. They sheathe their swords, but are still annoyed with each other. lines 23-63

3 **Falstaff's very ill**
Falstaff's serving boy asks Pistol and Nell to come and look after him. The Hostess goes with the Boy. Bardolph persuades Nym and Pistol to make friends again. The Hostess comes out and tells the men that Falstaff is in a really bad way. They all go in to see him. lines 64-104

Nell Quickly is <u>landlady</u>, or <u>Hostess</u>, of a London pub. This scene could take place in a street near the pub, or even just outside it.

> Please don't fight — your mate's ill.

> That's a flippin' big tear!

> Hey! Quit it lads — not now.

> Yeah, yeah, yeah...

> You cheeky back-swiper!

<u>Falstaff</u> has been friends with this lot for years. He's an important character in Shakespeare's plays about Henry V's dad, <u>Henry IV Parts 1 and 2.</u>

Before Henry was King, Falstaff was his <u>partner in crime</u> for drinking, carousing and general bad behaviour. Nell says Falstaff is ill because he is so <u>upset</u> about being <u>dropped</u> now that Henry is King.

What Happens in Act Two

**ACT 2
SCENE 2**

It's <u>no good</u> just having a <u>rough idea</u> of what happens. You need to know <u>who</u> does <u>what</u>, and <u>when</u> they do it. It's the <u>only way</u> to be sure you <u>really understand</u> the scene you get in the SAT.

Scene Two — Henry Calls the Traitors' Bluff

The English army is meeting up at <u>Southampton</u>, ready to sail across to France.

The punishment for <u>treason</u> is <u>death</u>.

1 Henry knows all about the traitors
Exeter, Bedford and Westmorland are at Southampton. Bedford is surprised Henry hasn't had the traitors arrested yet. Exeter tells him it will happen soon enough. lines 1-11

2 The traitors think they'll get away with it
Henry arrives with Cambridge, Scroop and Gray. He knows they're planning to kill him, but he doesn't let on yet. He asks the traitors whether they think the war will be successful. They all say they are sure it will. lines 12-39

3 Henry leads them up the garden path
He orders Exeter to set free a man who was arrested the day before for insulting Henry. Cambridge, Scroop and Gray all tell Henry it's a bad idea to be too soft on people who are a threat to him. Henry has the man released anyway. lines 39-60

4 Henry reveals that he knows about their plans
Henry has told the traitors they will have special jobs while he's away. He hands out letters which they think are about these jobs. In fact the letters tell the traitors that the game's up. They beg Henry not to be too hard on them. lines 61-78

5 The traitors are arrested
Henry says they can forget about mercy. He is disgusted with them, especially Scroop, who was one of his closest friends. Exeter arrests them all. They apologise to Henry, but he's not impressed and sentences them to death. Cambridge, Scroop and Gray are led away. lines 79-182

6 It's time to head for France
Henry tells the other lords with him that now the bad luck's out of the way he's sure the war in France will go well for England. lines 183-194

Why the dagger? — no particular treason...

Now, if you wrote about this scene — or any scene — in the SAT, you'd need to know <u>who</u> everybody is, and <u>what happens</u> to them later in the play. It's the best way to avoid making <u>dodgy</u> mistakes — <u>and</u> you'll actually find yourself with <u>tons more ideas</u> about what to write.

Section Six — Understanding The Story

ACT 2 SCENES 3 & 4 — What Happens in Act Two

The question you get in the SAT may only be about <u>one scene</u>, but to give a <u>full answer</u>, you'll have to know what happens <u>before</u> and <u>after</u> the scene you're writing about.

Scene Three — The Lowlifes are off to War

1 **Falstaff is dead**
Nym, Pistol and Bardolph are setting out for Southampton with Falstaff's servant boy. The Hostess wants to come with them as far as Staines, but Pistol tells her not to. He says he's too depressed about Falstaff dying and wants to concentrate on mourning. lines 1-7

2 **The Hostess describes Falstaff's last hours**
Nell says he died a good death. lines 8-36

3 **Pistol kisses the Hostess goodbye**
He asks her to look after his things and watch out for conmen. Bardolph kisses Nell goodbye too, but Nym says he can't because he's still jealous. lines 37-50

He's <u>still upset</u> about Pistol marrying her.

Scene Four — Defence Discussions at the French Court

...and here's the family tree to prove it!

That don't prove diddly, sunshine.

olden times French king

Henry King of France

1 **The French King's preparing for war**
The Dauphin thinks Henry's too young and new to his job to be a real danger. The Constable warns him to take Henry more seriously. The King points out that Henry's descended from Edward the Black Prince, who beat the French at Crécy. lines 1-64

2 **Exeter arrives with a message from Henry**
Henry wants the King to hand over his title and land. Exeter has brought a family tree to show Henry's heir to the French throne. If the French King won't hand over the crown Henry will fight for it to the bitter end. lines 65-111

3 **Exeter's got a message for the Dauphin**
Henry really hated the tennis-balls joke. He wants the King to apologise on the Dauphin's behalf. The Dauphin stands by his insult. Exeter tells him he'd better watch out. The King tells Exeter he will give him a reply for Henry in the morning. lines 112-147

My cousin Ash — a family tree...

<u>Good news</u> — you <u>don't</u> have to know all about <u>everything</u>. Don't <u>worry</u> about <u>Falstaff</u>. There's a lot of talk about him, but he <u>doesn't appear</u> on stage so you <u>won't</u> have to write about him.

What Happens in Act Three

Act 3 is where the action starts. If you were watching the play in a theatre you wouldn't see much of it because Shakespeare didn't have fancy special effects — it definitely gets more lively though.

Chorus — the English Force Sets Sail

In the last scene Exeter said Henry and the army were already in France. The Chorus backtracks a bit to give you a picture of the army sailing across.

O do but think
You stand upon the rivage and behold
A city on th'inconstant billows dancing...
(13-15)

1 **The audience need to use their imaginations**
The Chorus asks you to picture the fleet setting sail from Southampton. The fleet is sailing to Harfleur in France and looking really impressive. England seems deserted. Every man of fighting age has left for France. lines 1-24

2 **The army is fighting a siege at Harfleur**
The King of France has offered Henry his daughter Katherine and some dukedoms to try and buy him off, but it's not enough for Henry and the war goes on. lines 25-35

Scene One — Henry makes a Rousing Speech

Henry encourages his soldiers
The English cannons have broken through the walls of Harfleur. Henry commands his soldiers to charge through the gap and enter the city. He tells them to be fierce, to think of their parents and of England. He believes all of them have noble fighting spirit. lines 1-34

Harfleur was a fortified town on the French coast. Henry would have had to win Harfleur before heading inland.

Once more unto the breach!

Scene Two — Not All the Soldiers are Impressed

There isn't any actual fighting in this scene, but all the characters rushing in and out give the impression of action.

The Boy doesn't fight —he's too young. His job is to fetch and carry for Nym, Pistol and Bardolph.

1 **Not everyone's keen to fight**
Bardolph mimics Henry's speech. Pistol, Nym and the Boy say they'd rather be in London — it's too dangerous here. lines 1-23

2 **Llewellyn drives the men into battle**
The Boy is left behind. He wishes he didn't have to work for such miserable rascals, and says he doesn't want to be dragged into their criminal activities. The Boy leaves. lines 24-45

Scene Three — The Captains have a Row

1 **Gower says Llewellyn's wanted at the mines**
Llewellyn says the mines are a disaster. He blames Captain Macmorris. Just then Macmorris turns up with Jamy. He says the mines are a mess, but doesn't think it's his fault. lines 1-35

2 **Llewellyn wants to debate military technique**
Macmorris points out that they should be fighting not talking. A parley is sounded and the Captains go off. lines 36-76

In a siege, mines are tunnels dug under the walls and filled with explosives.

It's a mess!

So what? Let's fight!

A parley is a tune played on a trumpet. The French play the parley to let the English know they want to talk peace.

ACT 3
SCENES 4, 5 & 6

What Happens in Act Three

This is a good time to check you know the story so far. Go back to the beginning of this section and test yourself on each scene. If you can't remember what happens read that scene again.

Scene Four — Henry gives the Governor an Earful

Henry gets pretty nasty in this scene. He doesn't believe in a softly-softly approach.

1 **Henry goes to the walls of Harfleur**
He tells the governor this is his last chance to surrender. If he doesn't Henry will flatten the town without mercy. He won't be able to control his soldiers, and they will rape and kill the people of the town. lines 1-43

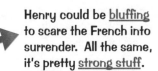
Henry could be bluffing to scare the French into surrender. All the same, it's pretty strong stuff.

2 **The Governor has to give in**
He's had a message that the Dauphin's army isn't ready to come and help yet, so he'll have to surrender. Henry leaves Exeter to defend Harfleur, and says he'll be taking the rest of the English army to Calais for the winter. lines 44-58

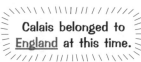
Exeter's supposed to stay at Harfleur, but he turns up in the battle scenes. It's probably a mistake by Shakespeare.

No really, I mean it...

Gulp!

Calais belonged to England at this time.

Scene Five — English Lessons for the French Princess

De foot, et de coun... Ah, I give up! Let's go for lunch!

Katherine's in a hurry to learn English because she knows her dad's promised Henry he can marry her.

Katherine wants to learn a few handy phrases
Her servant Alice has been to England so Katherine asks her to teach her some English. They start with the parts of the body. Katherine and Alice's pronounciation is terrible, but otherwise the lesson goes quite well. lines 1-55

Scene Six — The French Decide Henry's gone Far Enough

1 **The King's heard Henry's army is advancing**
The French nobles are really worried about looking like lily-livered wussies. They want to attack at once. lines 1-35

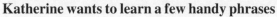
In Act 3, Scene 3, Henry said he was taking the army to rest at Calais for the winter. His army has to go through the middle of France to get there. The French think that's a bit too aggressive.

2 **The only thing they can do is fight**
The King orders the herald Montjoy to go and tell Henry to watch out. He orders his nobles to attack Henry's army and take him prisoner. The Constable thinks the English army is so small compared to the French that Henry will probably give up at once. lines 36-68

The French call the English "barbarous" and "bastard Normans". They're even rude about the English weather.

Har-fleur sec — I've just got to finish this siege...

Try not to get all dizzy here — the action keeps shimmying around from one place to another, from the French to the English and back again, and in between the different characters in the English army. The more you read the story the clearer it'll get — go on, try it and see.

What Happens in Act Three

I hope you're not forgetting you need to know the whole story. It would be really easy to make mistakes in your SAT if you didn't know what happens before and after the scene in the test.

Scene Seven — the Two Armies are getting Close

1 **Llewellyn's been fighting for a bridge**
He tells Gower that he was really impressed by Exeter and somebody called Pistol. lines 1-18

2 **Pistol hopes Llewellyn will do him a favour**
Pistol comes and tells Llewellyn that Bardolph's stolen a 'pax'. Pistol wants Llewellyn to talk to Exeter and save Bardolph from hanging. Llewellyn says there's no way he'll help. Pistol goes off in a rage. lines 19-52

3 **Gower tells Llewellyn Pistol's a dirty rat**
He says he's a conman who only goes to war so he's got stories to tell in the pub. Llewellyn agrees Pistol's not as heroic as he pretends to be. lines 53-79

4 **Henry and the army arrive**
He asks what's happened at the bridge. Llewellyn says the French have all been driven away. There were no English casualties, but Bardolph's got to be hanged. lines 80-104

5 **Montjoy brings the French war declaration**
The King's message says Henry is in big trouble. Henry tells Montjoy he doesn't want a fight now, just to get to Calais, but the English will fight and win if they have to. Montjoy goes back to the French King. Henry says that the English army will cross the river and camp there. lines 105-162

The English need to cross the bridge to get to Calais. The fight isn't between the full armies — just a few of the French and English.

A 'pax' is a religious painting. Bardolph must have stolen it from a church which makes what he's done even worse. The rule in Henry's army was that anyone caught stealing from the French would be hanged.

I think we only just got here in time...

Yes, his armies got very close for a second there!

Bardolph used to be one of Henry's drinking buddies, but Henry doesn't bat an eyelid at the news.

Scene Eight — the French are Dying to get Started

I don't need to even speak - just look at me... chic or what?

We're just cool.

My horse is cracking.

The French sound really overconfident in this scene.

1 **The French nobles show off**
The Constable reckons he's got the best armour ever. Orléans thinks he's got a cracking horse. Bourbon says his horse is the greatest. He can't wait for morning, and goes to put on his armour. lines 1-82

2 **The Constable's not impressed by Bourbon**
He says he's all talk. Orléans defends him. A messenger announces that the English have made camp close by. Orléans and the Constable think the English are brave, but they've bitten off more than they can chew. lines 83-139

Get lost Shakespeare — bard off...

Henry V has three main stories — one about Henry getting the French crown, one about Pistol, Nym and Bardolph trying to get rich quick, and one about the ordinary soldiers in the camp like Llewellyn or Williams. You'll be sorry if you concentrate on one and ignore the others — really sorry.

What Happens in Act Four

It's a long build up, but in Act 4 the clash between the English and French armies finally happens. The story gets a bit more complicated here — take it one scene at a time and you'll be sorted.

Chorus — the Night's Spent Preparing for Battle

The Chorus describes the camp better than you could ever show it on stage.

1 It's a dark still night
Through the darkness you can hear a low hum of activity, so quiet that the camp guards can almost hear each other whisper. Fires in each camp light the soldiers' faces. You can hear horses neigh, the armourers hammering. At three the clocks toll, and the cocks begin to crow. lines 1-16

2 The French are brimming with confidence
The soldiers are making bets on who'll kill and capture the most Englishmen and looking forward to morning. The English know they're in trouble, and sit by their fires thinking about the morning. lines 17-28

3 Henry does his best to keep English hopes up
He goes round the camp, talking to everyone. He doesn't show signs of worry or fear, and this gives courage to everyone he speaks to. lines 28-47

4 It's time to go to the battlefield
Obviously it won't be possible to recreate the Battle of Agincourt in all its glory. Once again the Chorus asks the audience to think of the things they see on stage as symbols. lines 48-53

And now, let's watch a fight...

Scene One — Henry goes Undercover

1 Henry's putting on a brave face
Henry is cheerful talking to Gloucester, Bedford and Erpingham. He says their tough situation is all the more reason to be brave, and jokes that at least they're all up early. He borrows Erpingham's cloak, and asks Gloucester and Bedford to get all the lords to meet up at the royal tent in a little while. lines 1-27

2 Henry asks to be left alone
Erpingham offers to stay with Henry, but Henry sends him off after Gloucester and Bedford. He disguises himself with the cloak. lines 28-34

The Chorus has got a bit ahead of the action. The battle hasn't started yet. This scene takes place at night in the English camp.

Look out...this scene carries over to the next page.

Chor-us — as the apples said to the knife...

Phoo-ee, Act 4, Scene 1 is enormous. If you find it's getting a bit bewildering break it down into chunks, and make sure you understand each chunk before you move onto the next one.

What Happens in Act Four

I hope you're not feeling tempted to <u>skim</u> a few pages. You've got to <u>read every page</u> carefully, and <u>remember the story</u>, if you really want to do well in your SAT.

Scene One — the First Person Henry Runs into is Pistol

3 Pistol demands to know who Henry is
Henry says he's an ordinary officer. Pistol praises the King in a rough and ready way. When Henry tells Pistol he's a relative of Llewellyn's Pistol curses him and wanders off. lines 35-61

Pistol says "Who goes there?" in <u>French</u>. He's worried he might have run into an <u>enemy soldier</u>.

4 Henry overhears Gower and Llewellyn
Llewellyn tells Gower not to be so noisy — he's sure soldiers weren't noisy in Pompey's camp. Gower points out that the French are being noisy. Llewellyn says that's no excuse. Henry likes Llewellyn's attitude. lines 62-81

Pompey was a famous <u>Roman general</u>.

Don't forget —
<u>nobody</u> recognises
Henry in his disguise.

5 Now he talks to Court, Williams and Bates
Henry says however scared people are they shouldn't show it. It scares everyone else. Bates wishes the King was here without the army — many lives would be saved. lines 82-110

6 Henry feels forced to disagree
He says he'd rather die fighting for the King than any other way as long as it's for a good cause. Williams points out they don't really know if it is a good cause. Bates says it doesn't matter — if they are doing wrong it's the King's fault. Henry says the King doesn't want his soldiers to die, and it's not his fault if they do. The others agree and tempers seem to be cooling. lines 111-178

7 Williams goes a bit too far
Henry says he's heard the King say he won't be ransomed. Williams says they'll never know if that's a lie when they all die in battle. They get into an argument and Henry challenges Williams to a duel. They swap gloves so they can recognise each other in daylight. The soldiers go off leaving Henry alone. lines 179-212

8 Henry's shocked at his responsibilities
He envies people who can live a simple, trouble-free life. lines 213-268

9 Erpingham finds Henry
He says the nobles are waiting at the tent. Henry says he'll be along in a minute. He prays, hoping for courage for his soldiers, and that God won't punish him for his father's sins against Richard II. Gloucester calls Henry and he goes off to face his nobles and the day. lines 269-290

The King won't be ransomed.

You're wrong! Take the glove or I'll deck you!

I'll take this till we meet again.

That's no way to talk to a king!

Henry's <u>father</u> was King too. He didn't inherit the crown though — he <u>overthrew</u> Richard II, who was later <u>murdered</u> and buried like an ordinary man. Henry had him <u>reburied</u> in the proper <u>royal style</u> and ordered prayers to be said for his soul.

Get tough with a diamond — fight a jewel...

If you're <u>not sure</u> who a <u>character</u> is look him up in Section 5 as you read the story. Knowing the characters'll <u>help you</u> write about the story better — and knowing the story'll help you write about the characters better. The better you know your stuff the <u>easier</u> it gets — and that's a <u>promise</u>.

ACT 4
SCENES 2, 3 & 4
What Happens in Act Four

Blimey, this play goes on a bit — well into Act 4 and we <u>still</u> haven't seen a battle.
This is where it <u>finally</u> starts though. Keep plugging on, and <u>get the story straight</u>.

Scene Two — *The French are Still Sure of Success*

1 **It's dawn on the day of the battle**
The French nobles call for their horses. They're full of fancy phrases, showing off their bravery. lines 1-12

2 **The English army is lined up ready for battle**
The Constable calls on the nobles to mount their horses. He says the English are so weak they will keel over when they see the French nobles. lines 13-36

3 **Grandpré wants to know what they're waiting for**
He says the crows will have the English if they don't hurry up. At last they ride to the battlefield. lines 37-62

Scene Three — *Henry tells his Men they'll be Proud of this Day*

1 **Henry has gone to check out the French**
Exeter tells the other nobles the French army outnumbers theirs five to one. Salisbury goes to the battleline. lines 1-16

2 **Henry returns from the field**
Westmorland wishes they had a few more men. Henry replies with a long and inspiring speech — the army should be pleased they are so few as it will be all the more credit to them when they win. Today is St. Crispin's day, and they will remember it with pride all their lives. lines 16-67

3 **Salisbury warns the enemy is about to charge**
The nobles dash off to their places in the battleline. Montjoy comes to give Henry a last chance to withdraw. Henry tells Montjoy he won't give up. York asks to lead the charge. Henry lets him and orders everyone to take their positions. lines 68-132

Scene Four — *Pistol takes a Prisoner*

The waggons and carts which carry the luggage are called the 'baggage train' in the play.

1 **Pistol's caught a nice juicy Frenchman**
Neither soldier understands the other and the Boy has to translate. Pistol keeps threatening the Frenchman. He promises to give Pistol lots of cash if he doesn't kill him. Pistol accepts and leads the Frenchman away. lines 1-52

2 **The Boy is left alone**
He says Nym's been hanged as well as Bardolph. The only reason Pistol hasn't is he's not brave enough to steal anything 'adventurously'. He goes to join the other boys looking after the luggage. lines 53-61

A holy potato-snack pub — St. Crisp-inn...

The action jumps <u>all over the place</u> in Act 4. Take it <u>one scene at a time</u> to make sure you soak it all in.

What Happens in Act Four

You probably thought <u>reading</u> this was bad enough. I reckon you need to <u>test yourself</u> too. After you've read about a scene <u>cover it up</u>, and tell yourself what happened <u>out loud</u>.

Scene Five — The French have had a <u>Nasty Surprise</u>

> The devil take order now! I'll to the throng. Let life be short, else shame will be too long.
> (22-23)

The French are in a complete mess
The Constable is on the verge of giving up. Bourbon is so ashamed he talks of suicide, then he calls on the nobles to throw themselves back into the chaotic battle — maybe there they can die with honour. lines 1-24

Scene Six — The English are <u>Doing Well</u>

D'oh

1 **The battle's not over yet**
Henry encourages everyone to keep going — the French are still fighting. lines 1-2

2 **Exeter brings sad news**
The Duke of York has been killed. He died alongside the Eark of Suffolk. Both men were dreadfully wounded. Before York died he asked Exeter to 'commend his service' to Henry. Exeter and Henry are both upset. lines 3-32

"Commend my service" means "tell him I am still his obedient and faithful servant."

3 **The French make a last-ditch attempt**
Henry orders the English soldiers to kill any prisoners they have taken in the battle. lines 32-38

This is a <u>cruel</u> decision to make. The prisoners' lives should be safe, and Henry is <u>breaking</u> the normal <u>rules of war</u>.

Scene Seven — The French are Getting <u>Desperate</u>

Oh dear, that's going rather against the etiquette of a friendly battle isn't it?

Yes, no wonder Henry's miffed!

<u>Alexander the Great</u> was <u>king</u> of a Greek country called Macedon in the 4th century B.C. Macedon was a tiny little place, but Alexander conquered <u>half of Asia</u> while he was still in his <u>twenties</u>.

Raaaarrgh! Come on and get us if you think your 'ard enough!

1 **Gower and Llewellyn are shocked**
Soldiers from the French army have attacked the baggage train and killed all the boys looking after the luggage. They also stole or burnt everything from Henry's tent. Gower thinks this is why Henry ordered the French prisoners killed — he sees nothing wrong with it. lines 1-10

2 **Llewellyn says Henry's like Alexander**
Both men were born at towns on rivers. Alexander killed a friend in a drunken rage, and Henry had a drinking companion — Falstaff — who he turned away. Llewellyn means to be flattering to Henry. lines 11-50

3 **Henry's furious at the boys being killed**
He sends a herald to tell the remaining French to come over and fight or give up the battle. If they don't the English will come over and finish them off. lines 51-61   /continued over the page

| ACT 4 SCENES 7 & 8 | # What Happens in Act Four |

Sorry to disappoint you but there's <u>no surprise ending</u>. The English win the battle <u>hands down</u>. In Shakespeare's day that's what the audience was <u>waiting</u> to see.

More Scene Seven — the French Give Up

4 **Montjoy asks for permission to collect the French dead**
Henry doesn't answer — he asks Montjoy whether the English have really won, as there are still Frenchmen galloping over the field. lines 62-82

5 **The French have given up and Henry has won**
He thanks God and names the battle after the nearby castle, Agincourt. Llewellyn reminds Henry that when his great-grandfather Edward III won a battle in France, the Welsh soldiers wore leeks in their hats, and still do on St. David's Day. Henry says that as a Welshman he wears the leek too. Llewellyn is proud of Henry's Welshness. lines 83-110

6 **The argumentative Williams appears**
Henry sends Montjoy and an English herald to count the numbers of the dead. Then he has Williams called over and asks him about the glove in his hat. Williams says he's sworn to fight the man who gave it to him. Llewellyn says he'd better keep his oath. lines 111-127

7 **Henry sends Williams on a made up errand to Gower**
With Williams out of the way he hands the glove Williams is looking for over to Llewellyn. He says it's a glove he took off a Frenchman and sends Llewellyn to see Gower too. Henry knows Llewellyn will try and fight Williams if he thinks he's wearing a Frenchman's glove. He sends Warwick and Gloucester to make sure things don't get out of hand. lines 128-172

Scene Eight — The Williams Problem is Cleared Up

1 **Llewellyn doesn't twig the trick**
When Williams sees the glove and challenges him, Llewellyn tries to have him arrested as a traitor. Warwick, Gloucester and Henry calm things down. lines 1--45

2 **Henry reveals that he's the man Williams wants**
Williams apologises and says he would never have been so rude if he'd known it was Henry. Henry lets him off and gives him money. Llewellyn imitates Henry's generosity, but can only afford to give Williams a shilling. lines 46-66

3 **The herald brings the body count**
Thousands of Frenchmen have died, but only a few of the English. They're delighted and amazed. Henry orders religious thanksgiving services, and for the dead to be buried. lines 67-120

Plumbers love St. David's day — leeks everywhere...

The story with Williams gets <u>really daft</u>. It's a bit of a <u>comedy interlude</u> to lighten the atmosphere after all the <u>excitement</u> of winning the battle. If you find it <u>confusing</u> read Act 4, Scene 1 again.

What Happens in Act Five

ACT 5, CHORUS, SCENES 1 & 2, EPILOGUE

The <u>end</u>'s in sight — just a <u>few</u> more scenes to go. When you've <u>finished</u> try telling the <u>whole story</u> to someone (your dog or your goldfish will listen if no one else will) to <u>test yourself</u>.

Chorus — Henry Pops Back to England

The next bit's too long for the stage so the Chorus sums up
Henry goes back to England. Everyone goes mad with excitement. The time comes for Henry to go back to France and make a peace treaty. lines 1-46

The Chorus does its usual trick of running <u>ahead of the action</u> — Scene 1 takes place in France <u>just after</u> the battle of Agincourt.

Scene One — Llewellyn Gives Pistol a Piece of his Mind

Eat leek!

1 **Llewellyn's wearing a leek in his hat**
Gower points out it's not St. David's Day. Llewellyn says Pistol's insulted him about leeks and being Welsh, and he's going to teach him a lesson. When Pistol appears Llewellyn beats him up and makes him eat the leek. Llewellyn gives Pistol a groat and goes off with Gower. lines 1-60

2 **Pistol feels pretty low**
All his friends are dead. He'll go back to thieving and boasting about his wounds. lines 61-78

Scene Two — Henry Cuts a Deal in France

1 **Henry and his lords arrive at the French court**
The French King and Queen hope the negotiations will go well. The Duke of Burgundy says France is in a mess, and the sooner things are sorted out the better. lines 1-97

2 **The lords go and negotiate — Henry chats up Katherine**
Henry will marry Katherine if the negotiations go well, and he wants to persuade her to like him. She's suspicious of this rough soldier, but he talks her round, and even gets a kiss in the end. lines 98-253

3 **The negotiations have gone well for England**
Henry'll marry Katherine and inherit France when the King dies. The Queen wishes them well. lines 254-357

I'm a bit of a rough diamond really!

Ooh, go on then, gi's a kiss!

Here, Harry: her Pop's agreed!

Cheers Unc. It just keeps getting better!

Epilogue — That's All Folks...

The <u>epilogue</u> is a short speech used to <u>finish</u> the story off.

The author's tried to tell the story as well as he could
Henry didn't have a long life, but he did a lot with it. He left a magnificent inheritance to his son, who was only a baby when Henry died. The advisors who ruled the kingdom for him lost France and got England into a bloody mess. lines 1-14

A cheerful Cockney tree trunk — an 'eppy log...

I <u>hope</u> you've been learning the story as you go along — if not now's the time to <u>go back</u> to the beginning of the section and <u>really learn it</u>. Knowing the <u>whole play</u> will <u>save</u> you in the SAT.

Revision Summary

Knock me down with a goose-feather quill — that was a whopper of a section. Trouble is you don't just need to read it, you need to learn it. Get the story of the play firmly lodged in that useful space between your ears. You might still be thinking you can get away with just understanding the scenes they give in the SAT, but believe me, you need to know the whole story. Test yourself with these questions. You can look back for answers to start with, but in the end you should be able to answer all the questions without thinking — never mind peeping.

1) Who's the Bishop of Ely's boss?

2) How do the Bishops plan to save the Church lands in Act 1, Scene 1?

3) What present does the Dauphin send King Henry in Act 1, Scene 2? Why?

4) What's upsetting Nym in Act 2, Scene 1?

5) Name the three traitors who get arrested in Act 2, Scene 2. What's the punishment for treason?

6) What warning does the Constable of France give the Dauphin in Act 2, Scene 4?

7) What port does the English fleet sail from? Where are they going?

8) Which scene does Henry ask his soldiers to go "once more unto the breach" in?

9) Who says they'd rather not be at Harfleur in Act 3, Scene 2?

10) What does Llewellyn say is a terrible mess in Act 3, Scene 2?

11) Where does King Henry want to take his soldiers to spend the winter?

12) Who teaches Katherine a bit of English in Act 3, Scene 4?

13) What does Llewellyn think of Pistol at the start of Act 3, Scene 6? Does he change his mind?

14) Which army seems more confident before the Battle of Agincourt begins?

15) Who lends Henry a cloak in Act 4, Scene 1?

16) What does Henry give Williams after they argue?

17) What Saint's day is it when the English and French fight the Battle of Agincourt?

18) What does the French prisoner promise Pistol?

19) Exeter describes how two people die in Act 4, Scene 6. Who are they?

20) Who does Llewellyn compare Henry to in Act 4, Scene 7?

21) How much money does Llewellyn give Williams?

22) What is Henry promised in the peace treaty with the French in Act 5, Scene 2?

What's your scene..?

Picking Your Task

It all looks a bit confusing at first. The main thing to remember is that you <u>have to</u> read <u>both</u> tasks <u>before</u> you can decide which one you're going to answer. That should get things <u>clear</u>.

You Get <u>Two Tasks</u> to <u>Choose</u> From

The <u>first thing</u> you've got to do is <u>read</u> through both of the tasks on <u>your play</u>.
Look at which <u>scenes</u> they cover — you'll <u>definitely</u> have studied one of them in class.

Pick a good 'un...

> You've <u>only</u> got to do <u>one</u> task —
> you need to do it as <u>well</u> as you <u>can</u>.

Pick the One You Can Do <u>Best</u>

You'll only have <u>two tasks</u> to choose from — choose the one for the scene you've <u>covered</u> in class.

There are lots of different types of task — but you <u>don't know</u> what choice you'll actually get in the SAT. You've got to be ready to answer <u>any type</u> of question.

You could get two tasks <u>like this</u> to choose from:

I've got two types of tusk.

Act 3 Scene 7, lines 1-103

TASK 5

In this scene Pistol asks Llewellyn to help him save Bardolph's life.

What do you learn about the character of Llewellyn in this scene?

You've got to <u>know</u> the scene or scenes well — or else you'll write a <u>dreadful</u> answer.

I haven't.

<u>Steer clear</u> of tasks where you <u>don't</u> really <u>understand</u> the question. You could lose a <u>lot</u> of marks if you don't answer the question exactly.

That steer's clear!

Act 4 Scene 3

TASK 6

In this scene King Henry speaks to his soldiers before the battle.

How does King Henry inspire his men to fight bravely?

Have a really good <u>think</u> about the questions — you <u>won't</u> have time to <u>change your mind</u> so you need to make the right choice.

Don't get caught out by questions that <u>look</u> similar to ones you've done in class. Use your brain and <u>check</u> for any sneaky little <u>differences</u>. It's the only way to do well.

Beware of different questions in similar disguises

Tasks are like noses — just pick your own...

The secret of doing well in Paper 2 is reading <u>both tasks</u> carefully <u>before</u> you choose which one you're going to do. You've got to do the one that asks about the scene you <u>know</u> well.

Reading the Bit From the Play

Once you've picked your task, you've got to <u>read</u> the bit from the play that <u>goes with it</u>.

Use these <u>Clues</u> to <u>Help you Read it</u>

This must be 'it'!

1) Check you've got the <u>right play and the right scene</u> — you really don't want to get <u>that</u> wrong.

HENRY V

2) These bits are instructions for people acting in the play — <u>nobody</u> actually <u>says</u> them.

Act 4 Scene 3

3) This tells you <u>who's</u> speaking.

Enter GLOUCESTER, BEDFORD, EXETER, ERPINGHAM *with all his host;* SALISBURY *and* WESTMORLAND.

GLOUCESTER   Where is the King?

BEDFORD   The King himself is rode to view their battle.

4) Here's what each person is <u>saying</u>.

WESTMORLAND   Of fighting men they have full threescore thousand.

EXETER   There's five to one; besides, they are all fresh.

3

5) This is the <u>line number</u>.

You Must <u>Read Through the Whole Thing</u>

It's boring, I'm afraid, but you've <u>got</u> to do it. You'll get about <u>six pages</u> to read. <u>Don't</u> try to skim it — you'll <u>miss</u> loads of important things if you do.

To The Stage

I'm lost - these stage directions are impossible to follow...

First, go through the passage <u>quickly</u> — just looking at the <u>names</u> of the characters and the <u>stage directions</u> (the bits that tell you what the characters are doing). Jot down some notes on who's in the scene and <u>what happens</u> — that's a good start.

Next, read through the <u>whole thing</u> carefully. Try to work out what it all <u>means</u> (Section 4 is all about <u>understanding</u> the <u>weird bits</u> in the language). If you <u>don't</u> understand some of the scene, don't worry — come back to it <u>later</u>.

You'll get <u>15 minutes</u> to <u>read</u> it and <u>make notes</u> — that's <u>loads</u> of time <u>if</u> you <u>don't waste</u> it.

<u>Invisible books — I can read right through them...</u>

Don't try to cut corners. The <u>only way</u> you're going to write a <u>decent answer</u> is by reading <u>right through</u> the bit of the play and finding all the things you need to write about. Harsh, but true...

Planning Your Answer

Phew — it all seems like a <u>lot of work</u>, but it <u>doesn't</u> have to be. It's all about <u>knowing</u> what you've got to do <u>before</u> you start writing. That's the <u>only way</u> to get <u>good marks</u>.

Check Exactly _What the Task is_ Asking For

Each task has a list of <u>handy tips</u> to help you with your answer.

Only four points? That's nowt...

> **What do you learn about the character of Llewellyn in this scene?**
>
> Before you begin to write you should think about:
>
> * Llewellyn's comments on Pistol's bravery at the start of the scene;
> * his reaction to Pistol's request to help Bardolph;
> * Pistol's response, and how Llewellyn answers him;
> * Llewellyn's report to King Henry, and how the King responds.

The examiners want you to write about <u>all four</u> of these points.

You <u>must</u> write about <u>these things</u> in your answer — don't miss <u>any</u> of them out.

That's an exact cheque!

Use the Handy Tips to Plan Your Essay

The <u>easiest way</u> to make sure your answer covers <u>all the handy tips</u> is to <u>make notes on all of them</u> as you read the scene. You can use the notes as your plan.

As you read the bit from the play <u>scribble notes</u> on each of the points from the task.

They can be as short and <u>messy</u> as you like — it's only <u>you</u> who has to read them.

You don't want to <u>run out</u> of things to say later — so <u>don't rush</u> into writing. <u>Take time</u> making your notes.

Stick to the <u>order</u> of the handy tips so you <u>don't</u> have to make a <u>separate plan</u>.

> _1. Llewellyn's First Comments_
> _He thinks Pistol is very brave - says "valiant as Mark Antony" (11-12): but he has been tricked ._
> _2. Response to Pistol's request_
> _Ll. says Bardolph should die, "if, look you, he were my brother": refuses help — "discipline ought to be used."_
> _3. Pistol's Response & Llewellyn's_
> _Pistol curses Llewellyn, but Ll. remains polite — Gower remembers P. is a rascal. Ll. says he'll wait till the right time - "that is well, I warrant you, when time is serve."_
> _4. Llewellyn's report to King Henry_
> _Ll. reports on bridge, and Henry agrees with B's death._

Make sure you write about <u>all</u> of your points in the 60 minutes. Keep looking at the clock to <u>check</u> there's <u>enough time</u> left.

> The SAT is 1 hour and 15 minutes long. Split it up like this:
> 15 minutes reading and taking notes;
> 60 minutes writing the answer.

Fingers — aren't they handy-tips...

The <u>handy tips</u> are there for a <u>reason</u> — so <u>don't</u> just ignore them. They're there to help you <u>plan</u> your answer properly. If you <u>don't</u> do what the task says, you <u>won't</u> get the <u>marks</u> and that's a fact.

Writing Your Answer

Once you've got a plan, you're ready to <u>start writing</u>. Write your answer carefully, though. Remember — you get marked on <u>how well</u> you write.

Write a Simple Opening Paragraph

Start by using the exact <u>words of the task</u> in your introduction. Your introduction <u>doesn't</u> have to be <u>long</u> at all. It's just there to show what your <u>basic answer</u> to the task is.

What do you learn about the character of Llewellyn in this scene?

In this scene you learn that Llewellyn is a brave and honourable character. He refuses to help Pistol save Bardolph's life when Bardolph is caught stealing from a church, because he believes Bardolph is a criminal. He also refuses to rise to Pistol's insults. At first, though, Llewellyn is taken in by Pistol...

Start by leaving a little <u>gap</u> — and do the same for <u>each paragraph</u>.

The first sentence uses the <u>exact</u> words of the task.

The second sentence explains your <u>answer</u> to the task.

When you've written your opening paragraph, just follow the order of your <u>plan</u>.

Use Lots of Tasty Quotations

Don't forget — quotations are bits from the <u>actual text</u>.

Whatever task you choose, you are <u>guaranteed</u> to get better marks if your answer's got plenty of good quotations. Trouble is, you've got to know how to <u>quote properly</u>. Here's how...

Copy down the <u>exact</u> words.

Pistol tries to speak as nobly as he can to Llewellyn, to persuade him to argue on Bardolph's behalf:

Therefore go speak — the Duke will hear thy voice — and let not Bardolph's vital thread be cut with edge of penny cord and vile reproach.
Act 3, Scene 7, 40-42

Leave a <u>line</u> of <u>space</u>.

Say <u>where</u> the quotation comes from. Give the <u>line numbers</u>. If there's <u>more</u> than one scene, give the <u>scene</u> number, too.

And tonight... Proudly presenting, Miss Penny Cord.

Don't quote <u>more</u> than <u>two or three</u> lines at a time.

If the quotation is <u>shorter</u> than a whole line, <u>don't</u> put it in a separate paragraph. But you <u>will</u> need to put it in <u>quotation marks</u>.

...Llewellyn refuses to help. He wouldn't ask for the Duke's pardon even if "he were my brother" (line 47)...

Weather forecasting — I need a rain-quote...

The examiners are <u>seriously keen</u> on quoting. If you don't quote at all, you'll get a <u>low mark</u>, no matter <u>how good</u> the <u>rest</u> of your answer is. Don't quote <u>huge chunks</u>, though — you only need a <u>couple of lines</u> to back up your answer to <u>each bit</u> of the task. Your quotes help <u>prove</u> your points.

Writing Your Answer

This is all about making sure you don't write a load of garbage — it's as <u>simple</u> as that.

Stick to the Point — Don't Just Tell the Story

You <u>don't</u> get marks for writing any old <u>rubbish</u>.
You've got to make sure you're <u>answering the question</u>.

Lots of people fall into a <u>terrible trap</u>.
They end up retelling the story of the scenes,
without actually <u>answering the question</u>.
If you do that, you <u>won't</u> get the marks.

Erm... I said 'a terrible trap'...

To make <u>sure</u> you're doing the task, keep the <u>words of the question</u> in your mind <u>all the time</u>.

Don't Contradict Yourself — It makes you look Stupid

Another <u>terrible trap</u> is saying one thing, then saying something which means <u>completely the opposite</u>. It makes people sound like they <u>don't know</u> what they're talking about.

King Henry agrees with Exeter's decision to execute Bardolph;
"We would have all such offenders so cut off;" (Act 3, Scene 7, line 98).
...King Henry knew Bardolph well, so he wouldn't want to kill his old friend, even if he was a thief...

Watch out — these two things <u>can't</u> both be true.

<u>Don't contradict</u> yourself — you'll <u>lose</u> important marks.

Finish Off Your Answer and Check it

You can make your work <u>even better</u> by making sure you <u>finish it off</u> well.

1) A definite ending gives you a chance to <u>sum up</u> all your points.
It'll <u>impress</u> the examiner, too. It makes your piece look <u>complete</u>.

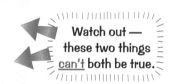

That's not quite what I meant when I said, "...finish with style..."

Llewellyn comes across as good and honest. He refuses to help Bardolph when he realises what he has done, and he doesn't lose his temper with Pistol, even though Pistol insults him. He reports proudly to King Henry about the fight at the bridge.

Your final paragraph can be <u>really short</u>, just like the opening paragraph.

2) Check to see that the <u>whole answer</u> is written in proper <u>sentences</u> and <u>paragraphs</u>. Check to see that all the <u>spellings</u> are right, especially the <u>names of characters</u>.

3) <u>Don't panic</u> if you run out of time. If there's a point that you <u>haven't covered</u> just bung down a <u>quick sentence</u> about it.

Don't disagree with a ledge — never contradict your shelf...

Keep clear of the two <u>terrible traps</u> (they're both on this page). When you've finished your answer, check through for daft mistakes — you <u>really</u> don't want to spell a <u>character's name</u> wrong. A clear <u>final paragraph</u> will help you pick up marks, but if you're pushed for time a <u>sentence</u> will do.

Revision Summary

A whole section of seriously useful tips for your SAT. You'd be madder than a pork pie not to learn that little lot. Use this Revision Summary to get it all remembered. If you're not sure of an answer, you can go back and check, but don't even think about going on to the next section until you're getting every last one of 'em 100% right.

1) Is it worth doing a task just because it looks easy?

2) If you don't understand a question, what should you do?
a) give yourself brain strain until you do understand it   b) give it a miss.

3) If a question looks similar to one you've done before, do you need to look out for any differences?

4) Can you avoid reading through the whole thing?

5) How much time do you get to read and make notes?   *a) 1 hour   b) a year   c) 15 minutes.*

6) If you don't understand a bit of the Shakespeare passage, should you forget about it, or should you come back to it later?

7) If the task gives you four handy tips to think about, how many do you have to write about?
a) none of them — they're only hints, after all   b) all of them — those examiners aren't kidding   c) one or two — you don't want to overdo it.

8) Do you have to do a separate plan?

9) Do your notes have to be: *a) nice and neat?   or   b) clear for you to read?*

10) Should you put an answer to the question in your first paragraph?

11) Should an introduction be: *a) long and rambling?   or   b) short and to the point?*

12) How should you put your main points in order?   *a) follow the order of the handy tips
b) at random   c) give them each a number.*

13) What guarantees you better marks?   *a) using quotations   b) sellotaping £20 to your exam paper   c) copying your answer out of the Oxford Companion to English Literature.*

14) Should you quote any more than three lines at a time?

15) If you quote less than one line, what punctuation marks do you need to use?

16) Should you check you've spelt all the names correctly when you finish your answer off?

17) What should you do if you run out of time?   *a) panic   b) write a quick final sentence.*

Writing About One Character

Here's the <u>easiest</u> kind of task you could get in the SAT. You've got to write about <u>one</u> of the <u>characters</u> in the scene. It's pretty straightforward — as long as you get the <u>method</u> clear.

Writing About One Character Isn't that Tricky

This is a <u>typical task</u> asking you to write <u>about</u> a character.

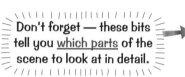

Don't forget — these bits tell you <u>which parts</u> of the scene to look at in detail.

Act 4 Scene 3

In this scene King Henry speaks to his men before the Battle of Agincourt.

How does King Henry inspire his men in this scene?

Before you begin to write you should think about:

- the fears of the English nobles at the start of the scene;
- how King Henry's speech in lines 18-67 gives his men confidence;
- how King Henry answers Montjoy's demand for ransom;
- the different ways King Henry uses language in his speeches.

Make sure you cover <u>all four</u> of them in your answer.

You Must Write about what Henry Says and Does

1) First look at <u>what</u> the English nobles <u>say</u> at the start of the scene.

> The English nobles seem worried at the beginning of the scene. They tell us that the French army is huge and fresh, unlike the English forces — Exeter says, "There's five to one; besides they are all fresh." (Scene 3, line 4). Salisbury replies it is "fearful odds", and the nobles say goodbye as if they'll never meet again alive. It is almost as if they don't believe they can win the battle.

2) Then look at how Henry <u>reacts</u> to what they say in a completely <u>different</u> way.

> Westmorland wishes that the English forces had "but one ten thousand of those men in England/ That do no work today" (Scene 3, lines 17-18). Suddenly Henry interrupts him. It is the first thing he says in the scene, and straightaway he sounds different. Instead of being negative and worried, he seems confident and jokey; "The fewer men, the greater share of honour" (Scene 3, line 22).

3) You've also got to write about the ways Henry <u>uses language</u> to inspire his men.

> Henry's speech is very poetic. He creates a vivid image of an old soldier who fought at Agincourt, and imagines how he will remember the battle in years to come:
> Then will he strip his sleeve and show his scars
> And say, "These wounds I had on Crispin's day." (Scene 3, 47-8)
> The language is poetic but very simple and clear. Henry uses alliteration between the words "strip", "sleeve", "show" and "scars", because it makes the description sound more beautiful. It's like a piece of word music to soothe his worried men before the battle.

Writing About Several Characters

This type of task is nasty — they're usually about <u>similarities</u> and <u>differences</u> between characters. The secret is to work out a lovely clear <u>plan</u> with <u>all</u> the characters <u>before</u> you start writing.

Make Sure You *Follow* the *Hints* Carefully

You need to work out exactly <u>which characters</u> you've got to write about.

Act 3 Scenes 1-2

In these scenes King Henry and his army are attacking the French city of Harfleur.

What are the similarities and differences between the attitude of King Henry and the attitudes of his soldiers to the war in these scenes.

Before you begin to write you should think about:

This <u>isn't</u> just about the characters — it's about what <u>they think</u> of the <u>war</u>.

- what King Henry says to his men in his speech in Scene 1;
- how Bardolph, Nym and Pistol talk and behave during the battle;
- how Llewellyn reacts to their behaviour;
- the Boy's comments on the characters of Bardolph, Nym and Pistol.

Make a *List* of the *Characters* and their *Attitudes*

Henry	=	*He is encouraging his men to fight bravely for honour — to show "That you are worth your breeding" Scene 1, 28.*
Pistol, Nym,	=	*cowards — "The knocks are too hot" Scene 2, 2.*
Bardolph		*the Boy says Bardolph "fights not," Pistol "hath a killing tongue and a quiet sword". All = thieves.*
Boy	=	*afraid; would rather be in a pub in London: "Would I were in an alehouse in London." Says the others are thieves & cowards.*

You Need to *Compare* the *Characters' Attitudes*

The way to get <u>really good marks</u> for this task is to write about the <u>similarities</u> and <u>differences</u>. In other words, you've got to <u>compare</u> the attitudes of <u>all</u> the characters.

King Henry's attitude to the war is positive. He tells his men not to be cowards, but to do their families proud; "Dishonour not your mothers;" (Scene 1, 22), and says they all have "noble lustre" — a noble look — in their eyes.

Immediately after, in the next scene, we see Bardolph, Nym and Pistol who aren't very noble at all. They are afraid to fight in case they get hurt. Despite all of Henry's noble speechmaking, they would rather be in the pub, as the Boy says, "Would I were in an alehouse in London" (Scene 2, 10). Their attitude is negative, unlike the King's.

Chopping up the cast — sever-all characters...

<u>Character questions</u> are about what the characters <u>say</u> and <u>do</u> in the scene — and how they <u>get on</u>.

Mood Tasks

Mood tasks ask how a scene makes you <u>feel</u>. They usually ask you to explain <u>how</u> Shakespeare gives a scene a particular <u>atmosphere</u>.

Mood Tasks <u>Look Tricky</u> — But They <u>Aren't</u> that Bad

The <u>key thing</u> about these tasks is how the members of the audience <u>feel</u> when they watch the scene, and <u>why</u> they feel like that.

Act 4 Scene 7 line 111 to Scene 8 line 65

In these scenes Henry plays a trick on Llewellyn and Williams.

Explain in detail how Shakespeare creates humour in this scene.

Before you begin to write you should think about:

All you have to do is look for <u>funny bits</u>.

* the way Llewellyn is talking at the beginning of the scene;
* what Michael Williams says to the King;
* how Llewellyn and Williams are taken in by King Henry's trick;
* how King Henry sorts everything out peacefully.

Focus on <u>How the</u> Audience Feels

You've got to write about <u>how</u> Shakespeare makes the audience feel a particular mood. There are <u>three big things</u> to look out for.

 1 Write about the <u>language</u> used in the scene — like whether it's <u>poetic</u>, or full of <u>silly words</u>.

These scenes are in prose, which shows straightaway that it is meant to be comic. In the first scene, Llewellyn speaks in a ridiculously heroic way. When Henry tells him that he has Welsh blood too, Llewellyn's reaction is funny because he is so joyful, and really over-the-top: "By Cheshu, I am your Majesty's countryman, I care not who know it. I will confess it to all the world."

2 Think how the characters could be <u>acting</u> — for example, to make it funny.

This is where you can really <u>pick up marks</u>. Most people <u>forget</u> to write about <u>acting</u> the scene on stage.

When Williams spots the glove Llewellyn is wearing, he instantly recognises it. Llewellyn seems a little confused at first, "Know the glove? I know the glove is a glove." (line 7). This is funny because Llewellyn doesn't realise what's going on. Then suddenly Williams hits him...

3 Look at how the other characters <u>react</u> to what's happening.

Warwick and Gloucester arrive just in time to stop a real fight. This is important because a real fight wouldn't be very funny. Warwick pretends not to know what is happening: "How now, how now, what's the matter?" One way of making the scene funnier would be if Warwick and Gloucester are both trying not to laugh at Llewellyn.

Comparing Tasks

Apart from comparing characters, you could also get asked to compare <u>what happens</u> in <u>two different bits</u> of a scene or scenes. This is a really <u>hard</u> type of task.

This Task's About Comparing Two Scenes

You need to go into <u>detail</u> — so give plenty of quotes from both scenes.

Act 4 Scene 2 and Act 4 Scene 3

In these scenes the French and English armies prepare for the Battle of Agincourt.

Comment in detail on the differences between the French army and the English army before the battle.

Constable and
Grand Prix

Before you begin to write you should think about:

You've got to <u>compare</u> the English and the French.

- the attitude of the French nobles;
- the speeches made by the Constable and Grandpré;
- the attitude of the English nobles;
- what King Henry says to inspire his army.

Don't Just Write About One Bit, Then the Other

The secret of <u>doing well</u> in these tasks is writing about the two scenes <u>together</u>. You've got to make the <u>differences</u> between the two really <u>obvious</u> to the examiners.

I'll huff, and I'll puff, and I'll blow you all down.

The French nobles are confident and arrogant before the battle. Bourbon and Rambures joke about the English soldiers weeping blood or tears: "How then shall we behold their natural tears?" (Scene 2, line 12). The English nobles, on the other hand, are worried about the size of the French army; "There's five to one; besides, they are all fresh" (Scene 3, line 4).

At the same time, the English are determined to fight well, and say goodbye to each other in case they die in the fighting; "Farewell, kind lord, fight valiantly today!" (line 12). The French are just in a hurry: "The sun is high, and we outwear the day" (Scene 2, line 62)

Each paragraph talks about <u>both</u> sets of nobles <u>together</u>.

Look at the <u>language</u> of the scene, and think about <u>how</u> the characters <u>act</u>.

In this scene, it's important that the Constable <u>only</u> talks to the French <u>lords</u>, but King Henry talks to his <u>whole army</u>.

The Constable's speech is ridiculous and arrogant. He says that the French could win just by blowing on the English army: "The vapour of our valour will o'erturn them," (Scene 2, line 23). He is only talking to the Princes, like Grandpré later. When King Henry speaks to the English, he speaks to the whole army. He tells them they are equally important on the battlefield, a "band of brothers" (Scene 3, line 60). Henry asks his men to be brave and heroic, while the Constable and Grandpré only mock the enemy.

Contrasting fruit — com-pearing...

With <u>mood tasks</u> and <u>comparing tasks</u>, always look at the <u>language</u> and how the characters <u>act</u>.

Tasks on How the Scene is Written

These tasks are all about how Shakespeare <u>tells</u> the audience something in a scene or a group of scenes. Remember to write about the <u>language</u>.

You <u>Have</u> to Do <u>Loads</u> for Tasks like This One

Be careful — these tasks are about answering the <u>exact</u> question.
If you don't, you won't get good marks.

Prologue and Act 1 Scene 1

One of the main themes of *Henry V* is the difference between the way things appear and the way they really are.

How does Shakespeare introduce different ideas about appearances in the Prologue and the opening scene?

This is tricky — it's about one of the <u>big themes</u> of the <u>whole</u> play.

Why Grandma, what big themes you have.

You're <u>not</u> just looking for one thing — you're looking for <u>lots</u>.

Before you begin to write you should think about:

- what the Prologue says about how the action of the play will appear in the theatre;
- why the Prologue tells us to use our imaginations;
- the way Canterbury and Ely talk about the change in Henry's character;
- the images used in the Prologue and by Canterbury and Ely.

It's about <u>How</u> Shakespeare Makes You <u>Notice</u> Things

Oh, I get you... So giant horses don't really exist...

That's right! They're just in your imagination.

1) Start by <u>finding</u> as many <u>different ideas</u> about appearances as you can. Then you'll need <u>examples</u> for each one — which means <u>quoting</u>.

> *In the Prologue, the Chorus tells us to use our imaginations because the events of the play can't really appear onstage: "Piece out our imperfections with your thoughts" (line 23). Straightaway he is telling us that things aren't what they appear to be — it's all a matter of imagining. When he says, "Think, when we talk of horses, that you see them" (line 26) the horses only appear in our imaginations, not on the stage.*

2) But that's <u>not</u> all you've got to do. The <u>exact</u> question is to explain how Shakespeare <u>introduces</u> these ideas about how things appear — how he <u>brings them into</u> the scenes and makes the audience <u>notice</u> them.

> *The Chorus speaks directly to the audience, so Shakespeare introduces the idea of appearances immediately. In Act 1 Scene 1, the two Bishops talk about King Henry's character in a similar way:*
> *And so the Prince obscured his contemplation*
> *Under the veil of wildness,* (lines 63-64)
> *Shakespeare shows us that Henry used to appear wild and careless, but that when he became King he changed. Ely is saying that Henry was hiding his true appearance all the time.*

False appearances in Henry V — not what they theme...

These tasks are <u>extra difficult</u>. You need to make sure you answer the <u>exact</u> question they ask you.

Writing As a Director

Here's a type of task that needs a bit more thought — writing as if you're directing a scene.

You Get Marked on Reading and Writing Just the Same

These tasks look completely different from the others, but they're marked on exactly the same things. They're about how well you read the scene and how well you write about it.

Act 2 Scene 2

In this scene King Henry uncovers a plot against him by Scroop, Gray and Cambridge.

Imagine you are going to direct this scene for a class performance.

Before you begin to write you should decide what advice to give the actors about:

- how you want King Henry to behave towards Scroop, Gray and Cambridge at the start of the scene;
- how you want Scroop, Gray and Cambridge to act towards King Henry;
- how they should react when King Henry reveals their treachery;
- how King Henry should show his anger towards them in his speeches;
- how King Henry should appear at the end of the scene.

It's about the actors — not just you.

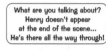

What are you talking about? Henry doesn't appear at the end of the scene... He's there all the way through!

You Need to Tell the Actors Two Things

(1) You've got to tell the actors how to say their lines — so you need to know what everything means.

Don't forget to quote the lines — or you won't get the marks.

> When King Henry gives Scroop, Gray and Cambridge their commissions, he says, "Read them and know I know your worthiness" (line 67). The actor playing Henry should look at the audience when he says this. He should sound completely sincere, but it must be clear to the audience that there is a double meaning to his words. He knows what they are really worth — nothing, because they are traitors.

(2) You also have to tell them what to do on the stage — how they should move around, and where they should stand.

Henry discovers the plot...

> As King Henry hands Scroop, Gray and Cambridge the papers that show their treachery, he asks them: "What see you in these papers that you lose/ So much complexion?" (lines 70-1) This means that the actors playing Scroop, Gray and Cambridge should go pale, and look shocked and afraid that Henry has discovered their plot.

Use the descriptions the characters say to help you tell the actors what to do.

How to guide the actors — give them the right directions...

Directing tasks can be really good for your marks. You've got to write how the actors should say their lines, and how they should move and behave on the stage. Don't forget to quote bits either.

Writing As a Character

OK, this is the kind of task you need to be really <u>wary</u> about. Writing <u>as if</u> you're one of the <u>characters</u> in the scene <u>looks like</u> a dead easy option. But the bad news is — it <u>ain't</u>.

It's About the Character's Thoughts and Feelings

You have to do <u>all</u> the <u>same things</u> as for any other task —
and you've got to <u>stay in character</u> as well.

Act 4 Scene 1

In this scene King Henry goes through the English camp in disguise on the night before the battle.

Imagine you are Henry.   Write down and explain your thoughts and feelings at this tense and difficult time.

You could begin: *It is hard to be King at times like these.*
Everyone blames you when things go wrong.

Before you start writing you should think about:

* Henry's worries about the upcoming battle;
* the way Pistol, Williams, Bates and Court talk about the King;
* the way the disguised Henry reacts to their criticisms;
* the kind of problems and pressure Henry faces as King.

You've Got to Write As If You're Henry

There's a real <u>knack</u> to these tasks — they're <u>not</u> as much fun as they look.

(1) You need to think about what the character is <u>like</u> and <u>how</u> he would <u>speak</u> — you have to <u>sound</u> just like him.

Those ordinary soldiers tried to blame the King for everything. If only they knew who they were talking to...

(2) You've also got to think about <u>where</u> these scenes <u>come</u> in the story.
Think about what Henry <u>does</u> and <u>doesn't</u> know at this point in the play.

Jean-Claude got a real shock from the English attack.

If you know Henry makes a good speech later in the same Act, you can make a <u>reference</u> to it. This shows the examiners that you <u>know</u> the play really well.

I know that we can win the battle tomorrow, as long as I can make a good speech to inspire the army. The French probably outnumber us, but that will make them overconfident. We need to take advantage of that to give them a real shock.

(3) The <u>hardest part</u> is making sure you <u>quote</u> enough.

I couldn't believe the rudeness of that soldier who thought I was lying about my ransom: "Ay, he said so, to make us fight cheerfully; but when our throats are cut, he may be ransomed and we ne'er the wiser."

I played a baker once — it was a bread role...

Remember — think about what the character's <u>like</u> and <u>how well</u> they <u>understand</u> what's going on.

Revision Summary

OK — that's what you're up against in the SATs. Any two of the types of task in this Section could come up in your exam. The secret is to be prepared for all of them. Don't go into the exam expecting one kind of task to turn up for a particular scene — maybe it won't. As long as you're ready for anything, you'll have a great chance of doing well. Have a go at these revision questions now — they're all about seeing what you know and what you need to work on. The more work you do now, the easier life'll be when you get to the real thing.

1) What do you need to write about for tasks about one character?

2) Do you need to cover all of the handy tips in your answer, or just some of them?

3) What do tasks about several characters usually involve? *a) retelling the story b) writing about similarities and differences between characters c) writing your own play.*

4) What should you do before you start writing your answer to one of these tasks? *a) have a cup of tea b) pray c) make a clear plan with all the characters.*

5) What do mood tasks ask you?

6) Apart from the language, what should you write about in mood tasks?

7) What kind of comparing tasks can you get asked to do apart from comparing characters?

8) When you do comparing tasks, should you write about both things together or separately?

9) In comparing tasks, what have you got to make obvious to the examiners? *a) that you like the play b) that yellow is your favourite colour c) that you don't like exams d) that you've spotted the differences between the things you're comparing.*

10) What are tasks on 'how the scene is written' about? *a) how the play ends b) how Shakespeare makes you notice things c) whether it's boring.*

11) Why are these tasks extra difficult? *a) you need to answer the exact question b) they smell.*

12) What two things do you need to tell the actors in directing tasks?

13) When you write as a character, do you still have to quote?

14) Why isn't writing as a character an easy option? *a) because it's in French b) because you have to do the same things as for any other task, and write as the character c) because you have to listen to hours of Europop.*

No more, make it stop!

Reading the Key Scenes

This section's got all the <u>most important</u> scenes from the play, and it <u>explains</u> all those fusty <u>old words</u> and <u>finicky turns of phrase</u>. You'll be <u>seriously glad</u> you read this when it comes to the SAT.

You Need to Understand as Much as Possible

1) You've got to <u>get to know these scenes</u> better than your own name. That way there won't be any <u>nasty surprises</u> when it comes to the SAT.

2) You <u>don't</u> want to spend half your reading time in the SAT wondering <u>what on earth</u> the characters are babbling on about. Use this section to <u>get a grip</u> on what the words really mean.

3) <u>Nobody</u> understands every single word Shakespeare wrote — not even the <u>crustiest old actors</u>. It's OK if you don't understand <u>everything</u> in the play. Just aim to understand <u>as much as possible</u>.

So, Crusty Actor Guy, do <u>you</u> understand Shakespeare?

Where are you? I can't see you through these stupid dark glasses.

These Little Bits are Here to Help You

The text's got lots of <u>lovely helpful bits</u> stuck on to make it easier to read.

The clouds give you a <u>quick overview</u> of what happens in each scene.

> The English are nervous. Henry makes a speech which gives them all courage. Montjoy asks Henry to give up while he can. Henry sends him away, and the English set out for battle.

It looks fine from up here, chief.

ACT 4
SCENE 3

Enter Gloucester, Bedford, Exeter, Erpingham with all his host,

Salisbury and Westmorland.

GLOUCESTER   Where is the King?

BEDFORD   The King himself is rode to view their battle.

WESTMORLAND   Of fighting men they have full threescore thousand.

EXETER   There's five to one; besides they are all fresh.

5   SALISBURY   God's arm strike with us! 'Tis a fearful odds.

command post   God be wi' you, princes all; I'll to my charge. If we no more meet till we meet in heaven, Then joyfully, my noble lord of Bedford, My dear Lord Gloucester, and my good lord Exeter,

10   And my kind kinsman, warriors all, adieu...

2 'The King's ridden out to see their army.'

3-4 '60,000'

7 'even if we don't see each other again till we're in heaven'

This is explaining <u>tricky words</u> from the text. The colour of the line numbers <u>matches</u> the colour of the text.

These boxes <u>explain a tricky word</u> in the text.

You expect me to make some kind of joke, don't you?

Read the key scenes — don't just lock them over...

<u>No shirking</u> in this section — or you'll <u>regret</u> it big time. If you don't <u>understand</u> the words of the play it'll be almost impossible to <u>write</u> anything in your SAT. It won't be easy at first, but you've got to <u>keep reading</u> through this section till you understand what's going on in <u>every scene</u>.

Left column notes

The Chorus introduces the play. It asks the audience to use their imaginations, as it's impossible to tell such a great story on an ordinary stage.

1-2 'make this play as creative as possible'

5-6 'then Henry, in his own distinctive way, would look as fierce as Mars, the Roman god of war'

8-11 'Please excuse the dull, uninspired spirits (the actors and writer) who've dared to try conjuring up such great events on an unworthy stage'

15-16 'a crooked little number in the most insignificant place can make a million'

17-18 'let us, who are nothing compared with the whole account'

20-22 'England and France, whose high cliffs face one another across the Channel'

23-5 'Use your thoughts to fill in what we leave out. Imagine each man you see to be a thousand, and imagine a mighty force'

30-31 'squeezing the achievements of many years into a couple of hours'

Squeeze it in!

PROLOGUE

Flourish. Enter Chorus.

CHORUS O for a Muse of fire, that would ascend
The brightest heaven of invention, *[spirit of inspiration]*
A kingdom for a stage, princes to act,
And monarchs to behold the swelling scene!
5 Then should the warlike Harry, like himself,
Assume the port of Mars, and at his heels,
Leashed in like hounds, should famine, sword, and fire
Crouch for employment. But pardon, gentles all,
The flat unraisèd spirits that hath dared
10 On this unworthy scaffold to bring forth *[round wooden theatre]*
So great an object. Can this cockpit hold
The vasty fields of France? Or may we cram
Within this wooden O the very casques *[helmets]*
That did affright the air at Agincourt?
15 O, pardon, since a crooked figure may
Attest in little place a million,
And let us, ciphers to this great account, *[zeroes]*
On your imaginary forces work.
Suppose within the girdle of these walls *[belt, circle]*
20 Are now confined two mighty monarchies,
Whose high upreared and abutting fronts
The perilous narrow ocean parts asunder.
Piece out our imperfections with your thoughts.
Into a thousand parts divide one man,
25 And make imaginary puissance.
Think, when we talk of horses, that you see them
Printing their proud hoofs i'th' receiving earth.
For 'tis your thoughts that now must deck our kings, *[dress]*
Carry them here and there, jumping o'er times,
30 Turning th'accomplishment of many years
Into an hour-glass: for the which supply,
Admit me Chorus to this history,
Who prologue-like your humble patience pray,
Gently to hear, kindly to judge, our play.

Exit.

Right column notes

The French King's paid three of Henry's most trusted men to kill him. They think they're getting away with it, but Henry has them all arrested.

3-5 'They look so calm; as though they were not only devoted to Henry, but faithful and loyal too'

6-7 'They've no idea, but Henry knows all their plans'

Bonjour, monsieur.

15-18 'Don't you think our army's going to cut its way through the French force, just as we have planned?'

You're all loyal, aren't you?

30 'wiped out their bitter feelings with sweetness'

33-5 'I'm more likely to forget what my own hand's doing than forget to reward people as they deserve'

36-8 'So we'll work all the harder, hoping to do you endless good work'

ACT 2 SCENE 2

Enter Exeter, Bedford, and Westmorland.

BEDFORD 'Fore God, his grace is bold to trust these traitors.
EXETER They shall be apprehended by and by.
WESTMORLAND How smooth and even they do bear themselves,
As if allegiance in their bosoms sat,
5 Crownèd with faith and constant loyalty!
BEDFORD The King hath note of all that they intend,
By interception which they dream not of.
EXETER Nay, but the man that was his bedfellow,
[spoiled] Whom he hath dulled and cloyed with gracious favours,
10 That he should, for a foreign purse, so sell
His sovereign's life to death and treachery!

Sound trumpets. Enter King Henry, Scroop, Cambridge, Gray, other Lords and Soldiers.

KING HENRY Now sits the wind fair, and we will aboard.
My lord of Cambridge, and my kind lord Masham,
And you, my gentle knight, give me your thoughts:
15 Think you not that the powers we bear with us
Will cut their passage through the force of France,
Doing the execution and the act
For which we have in head assembled them?
[lord]
SCROOP No doubt, my liege, if each man do his best.
20 KING HENRY I doubt not that, since we are well persuaded
We carry not a heart with us from hence
That grows not in a fair consent with ours,
Nor leave not one behind that doth not wish
Success and conquest to attend on us.
25 CAMBRIDGE Never was monarch better feared and loved
Than is your majesty. There's not, I think, a subject
That sits in heart-grief and uneasiness
Under the sweet shade of your government.
GRAY True: those that were your father's enemies
30 Have steeped their galls in honey, and do serve you
With hearts create of duty and of zeal.
KING HENRY We therefore have great cause of thankfulness,
And shall forget the office of our hand
Sooner than quittance of desert and merit
According to the weight and worthiness.
35 SCROOP So service shall with steeled sinews toil,
And labour shall refresh itself with hope
To do your grace incessant services.

Main text

KING HENRY   We judge no less. Uncle of Exeter,
Enlarge the man committed yesterday
That railed against our person. We consider
It was excess of wine that set him on,
And on his more advice we pardon him. **[40]**

SCROOP   That's mercy, but too much security.
Let him be punished, sovereign, lest example
Breed, by his sufferance, more of such a kind. **[45]**

[over-confidence]

KING HENRY   O let us yet be merciful.

CAMBRIDGE   So may your highness, and yet punish too.

GRAY   Sir,
You show great mercy if you give him life, **[50]**
After the taste of much correction.

[prayers]

KING HENRY   Alas, your too much love and care of me
Are heavy orisons 'gainst this poor wretch.
If little faults, proceeding on distemper, **[55]**
Shall not be winked at, how shall we stretch our eye
When capital crimes, chewed, swallowed, and digested,
Appear before us? We'll yet enlarge that man,
Though Cambridge, Scroop, and Gray, in their dear care
And tender preservation of our person, **[60]**
Would have him punished. And now to our French causes:
Who are the late commissioners?

CAMBRIDGE   I one, my lord:
Your highness bade me ask for it today.

SCROOP   So did you me, my liege.

GRAY   And me, my royal sovereign. **[65]**

KING HENRY   Then, Richard Earl of Cambridge, there is yours;
There yours, Lord Scroop of Masham; and, sir knight,
Gray of Northumberland, this same is yours.
Read them, and know I know your worthiness. —
My Lord of Westmorland, and uncle Exeter, **[70]**
We will aboard tonight. — Why, how now, gentlemen?
What see you in those papers, that you lose
So much complexion? — Look ye how they change!
Their cheeks are paper. — Why, what read you there,
That have so cowarded and chased your blood **[75]**
Out of appearance?

CAMBRIDGE   I do confess my fault,
And do submit me to your highness' mercy.

GRAY, SCROOP   To which we all appeal.

KING HENRY   The mercy that was quick in us but late
By your own counsel is suppressed and killed.
You must not dare, for shame, to talk of mercy, **[80]**
For your own reasons turn into your bosoms
As dogs upon their masters, worrying you. —
See you, my Princes, and my noble peers,
These English monsters! My Lord of Cambridge here,
You know how apt our love was to accord **[85]**
To furnish him with all appertinents
Belonging to his honour; and this man
Hath for a few light crowns lightly conspired,
And sworn unto the practices of France,
To kill us here in Hampton: to the which **[90]**

[plots]

This knight, no less for bounty bound to us
Than Cambridge is, hath likewise sworn. But oh,
What shall I say to thee, Lord Scroop, thou cruel,
Ingrateful, savage and inhuman creature?
Thou that didst bear the key of all my counsels, **[95]**
That knew'st the very bottom of my soul,
That almost mightst have coined me into gold,
Wouldst thou have practised on me, for thy use?
May it be possible that foreign hire
Could out of thee extract one spark of evil **[100]**

[crude]

That might annoy my finger? 'Tis so strange
That, though the truth of it stands off as gross
As black and white, my eye will scarcely see it.
Treason and murder ever kept together,
As two yoke-devils sworn to either's purpose, **[105]**
Working so grossly in a natural cause
That admiration did not whoop at them.
But thou, 'gainst all proportion, didst bring in
Wonder to wait on treason and on murder;
And whatsoever cunning fiend it was **[110]**
That wrought upon thee so preposterously
Hath got the voice in hell for excellence.
All other devils that suggest by treasons
Do botch and bungle up damnation
With patches, colours, and with forms, being fetched **[115]**
From glistering semblances of piety;
But he that tempered thee bade thee stand up,
Gave thee no instance why thou shouldst do treason,
Unless to dub thee with the name of traitor.
If that same demon that hath gulled thee thus **[120]**

[fooled]

Should with his lion gait walk the whole world,
He might return to vasty Tartar back
And tell the legions, 'I can never win
A soul so easy as that Englishman's.'
O, how hast thou with jealousy infected **[125]**
The sweetness of affiance! Show men dutiful?
Why, so didst thou. Seem they grave and learnèd?
Why, so didst thou. Come they of noble family?

Annotations

40-41 'Free that man who was put in prison yesterday for criticising me.'

43 'after talking to him'

46 'by putting up with him'

49-51 'Sir, you're being extremely merciful if you let him live after threatening a severe punishment'

54 'due to being in a state'

56 'crimes punishable with the death sentence'

Who's for the chop?

70-1 'What is it in those papers that has made you go so pale?'

Ooh, you've gone as white as a sheet.

78-9 'I felt merciful just now, but your own advice killed off that feeling'

85-7 'you know my love for him made me keen to give him anything which would reflect his honour'

91-2 'who owes me no less for my generosity than Cambridge'

95 'you who knew all my secret plans'

98 'would you have plotted against me for money?'

105 'two devils working in partnership'

110-16 'whatever devil it was that tempted you to do such dreadful things is praised for his skill in hell. All other devils that tempt people to do treason, disguise it with an appearance of goodness'

125-6 'You have infected the sweetness of trust with suspicion!'

177-9 'may God give you patience to endure the pain of your death, and make you truly sorry for your costly crimes'

186 'all the obstacles in our way have been cleared'

187-89 'Let's put our forces in God's hands, by setting them to work at once'

The English army's besieging Harfleur. They've just broken through the defending walls and Henry wants his men to fight their way into the town.

10-14 'let your eye peer out of your head like a cannon; let your brows hang over your eye like a battered rock towering over its base in the swirling sea'

21 'sheathed their swords because there was no more opposition'

Poor miserable wretches, to your death,
The taste whereof God of His mercy give
You patience to endure, and true repentance
Of all your dear offences. — Bear them hence. **180**
Exeunt Cambridge, Scroop and Gray, guarded.
Now, lords, for France; the enterprise whereof
Shall be to you as us, like glorious.
We doubt not of a fair and lucky war,
Since God so graciously hath brought to light **185**
This dangerous treason lurking in our way
To hinder our beginnings. We doubt not now
But every rub is smoothed on our way.
Then forth, dear countrymen! Let us deliver
Our puissance into the hand of God, **190**
Putting it straight in expedition.
Cheerly to sea! The signs of war advance.
No King of England if not King of France!

Flourish. Exeunt.

ACT 3
SCENE 1

Alarum. Enter soldiers with scaling ladders.
Enter King Henry, Exeter, Bedford and Gloucester.

KING HENRY Once more unto the breach, dear friends, once more,
Or close the wall up with our English dead. [break in walls]
In peace there's nothing so becomes a man [suits]
As modest stillness and humility:
But when the blast of war blows in our ears, **5**
Then imitate the action of the tiger;
Stiffen the sinews, conjure up the blood,
Disguise fair nature with hard-favoured rage.
Then lend the eye a terrible aspect;
Let it pry through the portage of the head **10**
Like the brass cannon; let the brow o'erwhelm it
As fearfully as doth a gallèd rock
O'erhang and jutty his confounded base,
Swilled with the wild and wasteful ocean.
Now set the teeth and stretch the nostril wide, **15**
Hold hard the breath and bend up every spirit
To his full height. On, on, you noble English,
Whose blood is fet from fathers of war-proof — [fetched]
Fathers that like so many Alexanders
Have in these parts from morn till even fought, **20**
And sheathed their swords for lack of argument.

Why, so didst thou. Seem they religious? **130**
Why, so didst thou. Or are they spare in diet,
Free from gross passion or of mirth or anger,
Constant in spirit, not swerving with the blood,
Garnished and decked in modest complement,
Not working with the eye without the ear, **135**
And but in purgèd judgement trusting neither?
Such and so finely boulted didst thou seem: [well-sifted, i.e. fault free]
And thus thy fall hath left a kind of blot
To mark the full-fraught man and best endowed
With some suspicion. I will weep for thee, **140**
For this revolt of thine, methinks, is like
Another fall of man. — Their faults are open. [plain to see]
Arrest them to the answer of the law,
And God acquit them of their practices!
EXETER I arrest thee of high treason, by the name of Richard Earl **145**
of Cambridge. I arrest thee of high treason, by the name
of Henry Lord Scroop of Masham. I arrest thee of high
treason, by the name of Thomas Gray, knight, of
Northumberland.
SCROOP Our purposes God justly hath discovered, **150**
And I repent my fault more than my death,
Which I beseech your highness to forgive,
Although my body pay the price of it.
CAMBRIDGE For me, the gold of France did not seduce,
Although I did admit it as a motive **155**
The sooner to effect what I intended.
But God be thanked for prevention,
Which I in sufferance heartily will rejoice,
Beseeching God and you to pardon me.
GRAY Never did faithful subject more rejoice **160**
At the discovery of most dangerous treason [acquit i.e. forgive]
Than I do at this hour joy o'er myself,
Prevented from a damnèd enterprise.
My fault, but not my body, pardon, sovereign.
KING HENRY God quit you in His mercy! Hear your sentence. **165**
You have conspired against our royal person,
Joined with an enemy proclaimed, and from his coffers
Received the golden earnest of our death; [promise]
Wherein you would have sold your king to slaughter,
His princes and his peers to servitude, **170**
His subjects to oppression and contempt, [value]
And his whole kingdom into desolation.
Touching our person seek we no revenge,
But we our kingdom's safety must so tender,
Whose ruin you have sought, that to her laws **175**
We do deliver you. Get ye therefore hence,

130-35 'moderate eaters, emotionally well-balanced, consistent, presenting themselves modestly, and not trusting in appearances'

137-9 'your disgrace spoils the reputation of the finest-seeming men'

You're under arrest!

156 'Thank God I have been prevented from doing what I planned'

163 'Please forgive my action, but punish my body'

You're in for it now.

Dishonour not your mothers; now attest
That those whom you call fathers did beget you.
Be copy now to men of grosser blood
And teach them how to war. And you, good yeomen,
Whose limbs were made in England, show us here
The mettle of your pasture; let us swear
That you are worth your breeding — which I doubt not;
For there is none of you so mean and base
That hath not noble lustre in your eyes.
I see you stand like greyhounds in the slips,
Straining upon the start. The game's afoot!
Follow your spirit, and upon this charge
Cry 'God for Harry! England and Saint George!'

Alarum, and chambers go off. Exeunt.

24 'set an example for cruder men than yourselves'

prove

26-7 'show us the strength that's in your land'

farmers

31 'you look like greyhounds straining at your leashes'

ACT 3
SCENE 2

Enter Nym, Bardolph, Pistol and Boy.

BARDOLPH On, on, on, on, on! To the breach, to the breach!
NYM Pray thee, Corporal, stay; the knocks are too hot, and for mine own part I have not a case of lives. The humour of it is too hot, that is the very plain-song of it.
PISTOL The plain-song is most just, for humours do abound.
Knocks go and come, God's vassals drop and die,
And sword and shield
In bloody field
Doth win immortal fame.
BOY Would I were in an alehouse in London! I would give all my fame for a pot of ale and safety.
PISTOL And I.
If wishes would prevail with me,
My purpose shoud not fail with me,
But thither would I hie.
BOY As duly,
But not as truly,
As bird doth sing on bough.

Enter Llewellyn.

LLEWELLYN Up to the preach, you dogs! Avaunt, you cullions!
PISTOL Be merciful, great duke, to men of mould! Abate thy rage, abate thy manly rage! Abate thy rage, great duke! Good bawcock, bate thy rage! Use lenity, sweet chuck!
NYM These be good humours! Your honour runs bad humours!

Exeunt all but the Boy.

servants (God's vassals)

Nym, Pistol and Bardolph aren't feeling heroic. They'd rather be at home. The Boy is really unimpressed.

3-4 'I haven't got a whole stack of lives. The fact is, this all looks a bit dangerous to me'

20 'men made of clay' (like Adam)

22 'Dear chicken, control your anger!'

BOY As young as I am, I have observed these three swashers. I am boy to them all three, but all they three, though they would serve me, could not be man to me; for indeed three such antics do not amount to a man. For Bardolph, he is white-livered and red-faced, by the means whereof 'a faces it out but fights not. For Pistol, he hath a killing tongue and a quiet sword, by the means whereof 'a breaks words and keeps whole weapons. For Nym, he hath heard that men of few words are the best men, and therefore he scorns to say his prayers lest 'a should be thought a coward; but his few bad words are matched with as few good deeds, for 'a never broke any man's head but his own, and that was against a post when he was drunk. They will steal anything, and call it purchase. Bardolph stole a lute-case, bore it twelve leagues, and sold it for three-halfpence. Nym and Bardolph are sworn brothers in filching, and in Calais they stole a fire-shovel. I knew by that piece of service the men would carry coals. They would have me as familiar with men's pockets as their gloves or their handkerchiefs, which makes much against my manhood if I should take from another's pocket to put into mine, for it is plain pocketing up of wrongs. I must leave them and seek some better service; their villainy goes against my weak stomach, and therefore I must cast it up.

Exit.

show-offs (swashers)

jokers

buying

ACT 3
SCENE 3

Enter Gower and Llewellyn.

GOWER Captain Llewellyn, you must come presently to the mines. The Duke of Gloucester would speak with you.
LLEWELLYN To the mines? Tell you the Duke, it is not so good to come the mines; for, look you, the mines is not according to the disciplines of the wars. The concavities of it is not sufficient; for, look you, th'athversary, you may discuss unto the Duke, look you, is digged himself four yard under the countermines. By Cheshu, I think 'a will plow up all, if there is not better directions.
GOWER The Duke of Gloucester, to whom the order of the siege is given, is altogether directed by an Irishman, a very valiant gentleman, i'faith.
LLEWELLYN It is Captain Macmorris, is it not?
GOWER I think it be.

siege tunnels (mines)

depth (concavities)

27-9 'Bardolph's a coward and a drunk, so he puts on a brave face, but never fights'

41-2 'I knew when they did that they'd no dignity'

44 'makes me less of a man'

Llewellyn wants to discuss military theory with Macmorris. Macmorris says now isn't the time — they should be fighting. While they're talking the French ask for a break in the fighting and talks.

This scene's all about how divided the English army is — these characters spend so much time arguing that they don't do any real fighting.

8-9 'By Jesus, I think the enemy will blow everything up.' Don't forget that Llewellyn's language is quite tricky — see P.25.

Section Nine — The Key Scenes

It's all kicking off here — Macmorris and Llewellyn are really winding each other up.

64-6 'perhaps I shall think you're not as polite to me as you really ought to be'

73 Remember that a parley is a trumpet signal which tells the enemy you want to stop fighting and have talks.

Llewellyn's been part of a successful attack on a French bridge. Pistol tries to get Bardolph off the hook. Montjoy brings a message from the French.

Llewellyn's speeches are full of images from ancient history and myths. They sound a bit ridiculous coming from him.

6-7 'generous and noble as Agamemnon.' Agamemnon was the Greek commander in a famous myth.

13 Mark Antony was a Roman general and politician. He was valiant, but Pistol certainly isn't.

14-15 'he's a man of no social standing, but I saw him do brave things'

LLEWELLYN By Cheshu, he is an ass, as any is in the world. I will **15** verify as much in his beard. He has no more directions in the true disciplines of the wars, look you, of the Roman disciplines, than is a puppy-dog.

Enter Macmorris and Jamy.

GOWER Here 'a comes, and the Scots captain, Captain Jamy, with him.

LLEWELLYN Captain Jamy is a marvellous falorous gentleman, that **20** is certain, and of great expedition and knowledge in th'ancient wars, upon my particular knowledge of his directions. By Cheshu, he will maintain his argument as well as any military man in the world, in the disciplines of the pristine wars of the Romans.

JAMY I say guidday, Captain Llewellyn. **25**

LLEWELLYN God-den to your worship, Good Captain James.

GOWER How now, Captain Macmorris, have you quit the mines? Have the pioneers given o'er?

MACMORRIS By Chrish, law, 'tish ill done; the work ish give over, **30** the trumpet sound the retreat. By my hand I swear, and my father's soul, the work ish ill done; it ish give over. I would have blowed up the town, so Chrish save me, law, in an hour. Oh, 'tish ill done, 'tish ill done — by my hand, 'tish ill **35** done!

LLEWELLYN Captain Macmorris, I beseech you now, will you vouchsafe me, look you, a few disputations with you as partly touching or concerning the disciplines of the wars, the Roman wars, in the way of argument, look you, and friendly **40** communication? Partly to satisfy my opinion, and partly for the satisfaction, look you, of my mind, as touching the direction of the military discipline, that is the point. [by the Virgin Mary]

JAMY It sall be vary guid, guid feith, guid captains baith, and I sall' quit you, with guid leave, as I may pick occassion; that sall I, marry.

MACMORRIS It is no time to discourse, so Chrish save me! The **45** day is hot, and the weather, and the wars, and the King, and the Dukes. It is no time to discourse, the town is besieched, and the trumpet call us to the breach and we talk and, be Chrish, do nothing. 'Tis shame for us all, so **50** God sa' me, 'tis shame to stand still, it is shame, by my hand; and there is throats to be cut, and works to be done, and there ish nothing done, so Chrish sa' me, law.

JAMY By the mess, ere these eyes of mine take themselves to slumber I'll dae guid service, or I'll lig i'th'grund for it. I owe God a death, and I'll pay't as valorously as I may, that sall I surely do, that is the breff and the long. Marry, I wud full **55** fain heard some question 'tween you twae. [two]

LLEWELLYN Captain Macmorris, I think, look you, under your

---

correction, there is not many of your nation —

MACMORRIS Of my nation? What ish my nation? Ish a villain, **60** and a bastard, and a knave, and a rascal? What ish my nation? Who talks of my nation?

LLEWELLYN Look you, if you take the matter otherwise than is meant, Captain Macmorris, peradventure I sall think you do not use me with that affability as in discretion you **65** ought to use me, look you, being as good a man as yourself, both in the disciplines of war, and in the derivation of my birth, and in other particularities.

MACMORRIS I do not know you so good a man as myself. So Chrish save me, I will cut off your head. **70**

GOWER Gentlemen both, you will mistake each other.

JAMY Ah, that's a foul fault!

A parley is sounded.

GOWER The town sounds a parley.

LLEWELLYN Captain Macmorris, when there is more better **75** opportunity to be required, look you, I will be so bold as to tell you I know the disciplines of war — and there is an end.

Exeunt.

ACT 3
SCENE 7

Enter Gower and Llewellyn, meeting.

GOWER How now, Captain Llewellyn, come you from the bridge?

LLEWELLYN I assure you there is very excellent services **5** committed at the bridge.

GOWER Is the Duke of Exeter safe?

LLEWELLYN The Duke of Exeter is as magnanimous as Agamemnon, and a man that I love and honour with my soul, and my heart, and my duty, and my life, and my living, and my uttermost power. He is not, God be **10** praised and blessed, any hurt in the world, but keeps the bridge most valiantly, with excellent discipline. There is an ancient lieutenant there at the pridge, I think in my very conscience he is as valiant a man as Mark Antony, and he is a man of no estimation in the world, but I did see him do as gallant service — [sub-lieutenant] [good fighting]

GOWER What do you call him? **15**

LLEWELLYN He is called Ancient Pistol.

GOWER I know him not.

15-16 'I'll prove it'

I know all about wars

29 'Have the soldiers digging the mines stopped their work?'

30 All the 'sh' noises are to show Macmorris is talking with an Irish accent.

36-7 'will you let me have a bit of a discussion with you'

43-4 'It shall be very good, in faith, good captains both, and I shall do as you ask, with good leave, when I choose to; so I shall'

53-4 'By the mass, before I sleep, I'll do good service, or lie in the ground for it'

56 'the long and the short of it'

59-61 'now and then he goes to war, so he can pretend he's a soldier when he gets back to London'

62-3 'they'll tell you, off by heart, where all the action was'

66-67 'they learn to reel it all off in military jargon'

71 'people who are an insult to the times we live in'

73-6 'I can see he's not the kind of person he pretends to be. If I find something to criticise him for I'll give him a piece of my mind!'

77-8 'I've got to tell him what happened at the bridge'

80-81 'have you come from the bridge'

83 'bravely defended the bridge'

84-5 'there was brave hand-to-hand fighting'

85-6 'the enemy had the bridge but were forced to retire'

91-2 'the Duke hasn't lost any men, except one who's got to be executed'

94 'all carbuncles and pimples and spots'

98 'dealt with like that'

Enter Pistol.

LLEWELLYN Here is the man.

PISTOL Captain, I beseech thee to do me favours. The Duke of Exeter doth love thee well.

LLEWELLYN Ay, I praise God, and I have merited some love at his hands. [hearty courage]

PISTOL Bardolph, a soldier firm and sound of heart, and of buxom valour, hath, by cruel fate and giddy Fortune's fickle wheel, that goddess blind that stands upon the rolling restless stone — [excuse me]

LLEWELLYN By your patience, Ancient Pistol: Fortune is painted plind, with a muffler afore her eyes, to signify to you that Fortune is plind; and she is painted also with a wheel, to signify to you, which is the moral of it, that she is turning, and inconstant, and mutability, and variation; and her foot, look you, is fixed upon a spherical stone, which rolls, and rolls, and rolls. In good truth, the poet makes a most excellent description of it: Fortune is an excellent moral. [lesson]

PISTOL Fortune is Bardolph's foe, and frowns on him, for he hath stolen a pax, and hangèd must 'a be, a damnèd death! Let gallows gape for dog; let man go free, and let not hemp his windpipe suffocate! But Exeter hath given the doom of death for pax of little price. Therefore go speak — the Duke will hear thy voice — and let not Bardolph's vital thread be cut with edge of penny cord and vile reproach. Speak, Captain, for his life, and I will thee requite. [pay back]

LLEWELLYN Ancient Pistol, I do partly understand your meaning.

PISTOL Why then, rejoice therefore.

LLEWELLYN Certainly, Ancient, it is not a thing to rejoice at; for if, look you, he were my brother, I would desire the Duke to use his good pleasure and put him to execution; for discipline ought to be used.

PISTOL Die and be damned, and *fico* for thy friendship! [fake]

LLEWELLYN It is well.

PISTOL The fig of Spain!

Exit.

LLEWELLYN Very good.

GOWER Why, this is an arrant counterfeit rascal, I remember him now — a bawd, a cutpurse.

LLEWELLYN I'll assure you 'a uttered as prave words at the pridge as you shall see in a summer's day. But it is very well; what he has spoke to me, that is well, I warrant you, when time is serve. [simpleton]

GOWER Why, 'tis a gull, a fool, a rogue, that now and then goes

20
25
30
35
40
45
50
55

---

to the wars to grace himself at his return into London under the form of a soldier. And such fellows are perfect in the great commanders' names and they will learn you by rote where services were done: at such and such a sconce, at such a breach, at such a convoy; who came off bravely, who was shot, who disgraced; what terms the enemy stood on. And this they con perfectly in the phrase of war, which they trick up with new-tuned oaths; and what a beard of the general's cut and a horrid suit of the camp will do among foaming bottles and ale-washed wits is wonderful to be thought on. But you must learn to know such slanders of the age, or else you may be marvellously mistook. [fort] [armed escort]

LLEWELLYN I tell you what, Captain Gower: I do perceive he is not the man that he would gladly make show to the world he is. If I find a hole in his coat, I will tell him my mind.

Drum within.

Hark you the King is coming, and I must speak with him from the pridge.

Drum and colours. Enter King Henry, with his poor soldiers and Gloucester.

God pless your majesty!

KING HENRY How now, Llewellyn, cam'st thou from the bridge?

LLEWELLYN Ay, so please your majesty. The Duke of Exeter has very gallantly maintained the pridge. The French is gone off, look you, and there is gallant and most prave passages. Marry, th'athversay was have possession of the pridge, but he is enforced to retire, and the Duke of Exeter is master of the pridge. I can tell your majesty, the Duke is a prave man.

KING HENRY What men have you lost, Llewellyn? [losses]

LLEWELLYN The perdition of th'athversary hath been very great, reasonable great. Marry, for my part, I think the Duke hath lost never a man, but one that is like to be executed for robbing a church, one Bardolph, if your majesty know the man. His face is all bubuncles, and whelks, and knobs, and flames o'fire, and his lips blows at his nose, and it is like a coal of fire, sometimes plue and sometimes red; but his nose is executed and his fire's out.

KING HENRY We would have all such offenders so cut off; and we give express charge that in our marches through the country there be nothing compelled from the villages, nothing taken but paid for, none of the French upbraided [forced]

60
65
70
75
80
85
90
95
100

22-3 'I have done things to deserve his affection'

25 Fortune was believed to be a woman spinning a wheel — sometimes up, and sometimes down.

36-7 'Fortune's against Bardolph. He stole a pax, and he's going to be hanged' A pax was a bit of metal with a cross stamped on it, used in church services.

41-2 'don't let Bardolph's life be cut short with cheap rope, and a horrible punishment'

46-8 'even if he was my brother I'd want the Duke to execute him'

50 'a fig for your friendship' To give someone the fig you put your thumb between your teeth.

55 'a pimp and a pickpocket'

56-7 'he sounded brave as anything at the bridge'

57-8 'I'll get even with him for what he said soon enough'

Main text (continued):

or abused in disdainful language; for when lenity and cruelty play for a kingdom, the gentler gamester is the soonest winner.

Tucket. Enter Montjoy.

MONTJOY You know me by my habit.

105 KING HENRY Well then, I know thee: what shall I know of thee?

MONTJOY My master's mind.

KING HENRY Unfold it.

MONTJOY Thus says my king: 'Say thou to Harry of England,

110 though we seemed dead, we did but sleep. Advantage is a better soldier than rashness. Tell him we could have rebuked him at Harfleur, but that we thought not good to bruise an injury till it were full ripe. Now we speak upon our cue, and our voice is imperial: England shall repent his

115 folly, see his weakness, and admire our sufferance. Bid him therefore consider of his ransom, which must proportion the losses we have borne, the subjects we have lost, the disgrace we have digested; which in weight to reanswer, his pettiness would bow under. For our losses, his

120 exchequer is too poor; for th'effusion of our blood, the muster of his kingdom too faint a number; and for our disgrace, his own person kneeling at our feet but a weak and worthless satisfaction. To this add defiance; and tell him, for conclusion — he hath betrayed his followers,

125 whose condemnation is pronounced.' So far my king and master, so much my office.   `certain`

KING HENRY What is thy name? I know thy quality.

MONTJOY Montjoy.

KING HENRY Thou dost thy office fairly. Turn thee back,

130 And tell thy king I do not seek him now,
But could be willing to march on to Calais   `truth`
Without impeachment: for, to say the sooth,
Though 'tis no wisdom to confess so much
Unto an enemy of craft and vantage,

135 My people are with sickness much enfeebled,
My numbers lessened, and those few I have
Almost no better than so many French,
Who when they were in health, I tell thee, Herald,
I thought upon one pair of English legs

140 Did march three Frenchmen. Yet forgive me, God,   `horse's lower legs`
That I do brag thus! This your air of France
Hath blown that vice in me. I must repent.
Go therefore, tell thy master here I am;
My ransom is this frail and worthless trunk;

145 My army but a weak and sickly guard.
Yet, God before, tell him we will come on,

Though France himself and such another neighbour
Stand in our way.

Gives a purse.

There's for thy labour, Montjoy.
Go, bid thy master well advise himself.
If we may pass, we will; if we be hindered,

150 We shall your tawny ground with your red blood
Discolour. And so, Montjoy, fare you well.
The sum of all our answer is but this:
We would not seek a battle as we are;

155 Nor as we are, we say, we will not shun it.
So tell your master.

MONTJOY I shall deliver so. Thanks to your highness.

Exit.

GLOUCESTER I hope they will not come upon us now.

KING HENRY We are in God's hand, brother, not in theirs.

160 March to the bridge. It now draws toward night.
Beyond the river we'll encamp ourselves,
And on tomorrow. Bid them march away.

Exeunt.

**ACT 3
SCENE 8**

Enter the Constable of France, the Lord Rambures, Orléans, Bourbon and others.

CONSTABLE Tut! I have the best armour of the world. Would it were day!

ORLÉANS You have an excellent armour; but let my horse have his due.

5 CONSTABLE It is the best horse of Europe.

ORLÉANS Will it never be morning?

BOURBON My Lord of Orléans, and my Lord High Constable, you talk of horse and armour?

ORLÉANS You are as well provided of both as any prince in

10 the world.

BOURBON What a long night is this! I will not change my horse with any that treads but on four pasterns. Ch'ha! He bounds from the earth as if his entrails were hairs — *le cheval volant*, the Pegasus, *qui a les narines de feu!* When

15 I bestride him, I soar, I am a hawk. He trots the air. The earth sings when he touches it; the basest horn of his hoof is more musical than the pipe of Hermes.

Margin notes:

148 By giving Montjoy the purse Henry shows he's above all the insults.

150-52 'If anyone tries to stop us we'll turn your brown earth red with your blood'

154-5 'we're in no state to fight, but we won't try and get out of it'

He means it.

All the French do in this scene is show off and quarrel. It makes them look ridiculous.

The night before the battle the French are longing for morning — they're sure they'll win.

1-2 'I wish it was day'

13-14 'He leaps from the earth as though his insides were hairs — *the flying horse*, the Pegasus, *with nostrils of fire!* Pegasus was a flying horse in the ancient Greek myths.

17 Hermes was a Greek god who charmed a terrible monster called the Argus to sleep, with the music of his pipe.

102-4 'when kindness and cruelty compete for a kingdom, the gentler one is sure to win'

105 'My uniform tells you who I am.' This is a very rude way to greet a king.

112-13 'we thought it best not to squeeze the spot till it was ready'

115 'admire the way we've held back till now'

116 If Henry lost the battle he'd have to pay a ransom for his freedom — Montjoy's saying he'll definitely lose.

119-21 'his treasury's too poor to pay our losses; all the men in his kingdom too few to pay back the men we've lost'

129-132 'You do your job well. Go back and tell the King I don't want to fight him now — I'd like to go into Calais without any trouble'

134 'a cunning enemy with a tactical advantage'

136-7 'the few men I've got left are only a bit more useful than the same number of Frenchmen would be'

142 'has puffed me up with that bad habit'

144 'all you're getting for a ransom is my body'

146 'with God before us'

Left margin notes:

19 'he's got a hot and spicy temper'

20 Perseus was the Greek hero who rode the flying horse Pegasus.

26-7 'he neighs like a king giving orders, and his face demands respect'

29-30 'from sunrise to sunset'

31-4 'If you turned all the sand in the world into tongues talking about my horse, they wouldn't run out of things to talk about. He's fit for a king to discuss, and for a king of kings to ride'

38-62 Orléans tries to wind Bourbon up, saying he goes on about his horse as if it was his mistress. Bourbon gets back at Orléans with double-edged comments about his mistress.

48-50 'you rode like an Irish peasant, in skin-tight trousers' He's suggesting the Constable wasn't wearing any trousers.

53 Bogs could also mean diseased women.

56 'At least my mistress (horse) doesn't have to wear a wig'

59-60 'That saying's as relevant as "The dog goes back to his own vomit, and the washed sow goes back to wallowing"'

Right margin notes:

63-4 The jibes have gone on long enough, and Rambures changes the subject.

66 'I hope some of the stars on your armour will get knocked off in battle'

67 'But I will keep my honour'

75-6 'I won't agree in case I can't keep my word'

78-9 'Who'll bet me twenty prisoners on a game of dice?' He means the winner in the game can have the ransom money from twenty of the loser's prisoners.

82 'I'll go and put my armour on.' There was a lot of armour to put on so it could take a long time — but not all night.

84 Rambures exaggerates to flatter Bourbon.

85 The Constable exaggerates even more to mock Bourbon.

88 'He's the busiest man in France.' Orléans could be defending Bourbon, or taking the mickey too.

89 'He's always doing something.' The Constable implies he doesn't actually achieve much.

98 'He doesn't need to worry about people knowing he's brave — it's no secret'

100 'His bravery's hooded like a falcon — take the hood off and it flaps its wings'

Play text:

ORLÉANS He's of the colour of the nutmeg. *[reddish-brown]*

BOURBON And of the heat of the ginger. It is a beast for Perseus. He is pure air and fire; and the dull elements of earth and water never appear in him, but only in patient stillness while his rider mounts him. He is indeed a horse, and all other jades you may call beasts. *[old nags]*

CONSTABLE Indeed, my lord, it is a most absolute and excellent horse. *[horses]*

BOURBON It is the prince of palfreys; his neigh is like the bidding of a monarch, and his countenance enforces homage.

ORLÉANS No more, cousin.

BOURBON Nay, the man hath no wit that cannot, from the rising of the lark to the lodging of the lamb, vary deserved praise on my palfrey. It is a theme as fluent as the sea. Turn the sands into eloquent tongues, and my horse is argument for them all. 'Tis a subject for a sovereign to reason on, and for a sovereign's sovereign to ride on, and for the world, familiar to us and unknown, to lay apart their particular functions and wonder at him. I once writ a sonnet in his praise, and began thus: 'Wonder of nature' — *[eloquent and flowing]*

ORLÉANS I have heard a sonnet begin so to one's mistress.

BOURBON Then did they imitate that which I composed to my courser, for my horse is my mistress.

ORLÉANS Your mistress bears well.

BOURBON Me well, which is the prescript praise and perfection of a good and particular mistress.

CONSTABLE Nay, for me thought yesterday your mistress shrewdly shook your back. *[viciously]*

BOURBON So perhaps did yours.

CONSTABLE Mine was not bridled.

BOURBON O then belike she was old and gentle, and you rode like a kern of Ireland, your French hose off, and in your strait strossers.

CONSTABLE You have good judgement in horsemanship.

BOURBON Be warned by me, then: they that ride so, and ride not warily, fall into foul bogs. I had rather have my horse to my mistress.

CONSTABLE I had as lief have my mistress a jade.

BOURBON I tell thee, Constable, my mistress wears his own hair.

CONSTABLE I could make as true a boast as that, if I had a sow as my mistress.

BOURBON 'Le chien est retourné a son propre vomissement, et la truie lavée au bourbier.' Thou mak'st use of anything.

65 CONSTABLE Yet do I not use my horse for my mistress or any such proverb so little kin to the purpose.

RAMBURES My Lord Constable, the armour that I saw in your tent tonight, are those stars or suns upon it?

CONSTABLE Stars, my lord.

BOURBON Some of them will fall tomorrow, I hope.

CONSTABLE And yet my sky shall not want.

70 BOURBON That may be, for you bear a many superfluously, and 'twere more honour some were away.

CONSTABLE Even as your horse bears your praises, who would trot as well were some of your brags dismounted.

BOURBON Would I were able to load him with his desert! Will it never be day? I will trot tomorrow a mile, and my way shall be paved with English faces.

75 CONSTABLE I will not say so, for fear I should be faced out of my way; but I would it were morning, for I would fain be about the ears of the English.

RAMBURES Who will go to hazard with me for twenty prisoners?

80 CONSTABLE You must first go yourself to hazard, ere you have them.

BOURBON 'Tis midnight: I'll go arm myself.

Exit

ORLÉANS The Duke of Bourbon longs for morning.

RAMBURES He longs to eat the English.

85 CONSTABLE I think he will eat all he kills.

ORLÉANS By the white hand of my lady, he's a gallant prince.

CONSTABLE Swear by her foot, that she may tread out the oath.

ORLÉANS He is simply the most active gentleman of France.

CONSTABLE Doing is activity, and he will still be doing.

90 ORLÉANS He never did harm, that I heard of.

CONSTABLE Nor will do none tomorrow; he will keep that good name still.

ORLÉANS I know him to be valiant.

CONSTABLE I was told that, by one that knows him better than you.

95 ORLÉANS What's he?

CONSTABLE Marry, he told me so himself, and he said he cared not who knew it.

ORLÉANS He needs not; it is no hidden virtue in him.

100 CONSTABLE By my faith, sir, but it is: never anybody saw it but his lackey. 'Tis a hooded valour, and when it appears it will bate. *[servant]*

Section Nine — The Key Scenes

> The Chorus describes the two camps waiting for morning. Henry passes amongst the English troops, giving them courage.

ACT 4
CHORUS

Enter Chorus

CHORUS Now entertain conjecture of a time
When creeping murmur and the poring dark
Fills the wide vessel of the universe.
From camp to camp, through the foul womb of night
The hum of either army stilly sounds,   5
That the fixed sentinels almost receive
The secret whispers of each other's watch.
Fire answers fire, and through their paly flames   **[pale]**
Each battle sees the other's umbered face.
Steed threatens steed, in high and boastful neighs,   10
Piercing the night's dull ear; and from the tents
The armourers, accomplishing the knights,
With busy hammers closing rivets up,
Give dreadful note of preparation.
The country cocks do crow, the clocks do toll,   15
And the third hour of drowsy morning name.
Proud of their numbers, and secure in soul,
The confident and over-lusty French   **[confident]**
Do the low-rated English play at dice,
And chide the cripple tardy-gaited night   20
Who like a foul and ugly witch doth limp
So tediously away. The poor condemnèd English,
Like sacrifices, by their watchful fires
Sit patiently, and inly ruminate
The morning's danger; and their gesture sad,   25
Investing lank-lean cheeks and war-torn coats,   **[ragged]**
Presenteth them unto the gazing moon
So many horrid ghosts. O now, who will behold
The royal Captain of this ruined band
Walking from watch to watch, from tent to tent,   30
Let him cry, 'Praise and glory on his head!'
For forth he goes and visits all his host,
Bids them good morrow with a modest smile,
And calls them brothers, friends and countrymen.
Upon his royal face there is no note   35
How dread an army hath enrounded him,   **[surrounded]**
Nor doth he dedicate one jot of colour
Unto the weary and all-watched night,
But freshly looks, and overbears attaint
With cheerful semblance and sweet majesty,   40
That every wretch, pining and pale before,
Beholding him, plucks comfort from his looks.
A largess universal, like the sun,   **[generosity]**

Right-margin glossary:

1 'imagine'
2 'darkness so black you have to strain to see'
6 'so that'
9 'each army sees the other's dusky face'
12-13 'equipping the knights, with busy hammers closing up their armour'
18-22 'The confident and over-eager French play dice to divide up what they hope they'll win from the English, and scold the slow-moving cripple night, who limps tediously away like a foul and ugly witch'
24-25 'think about the dangers tomorrow will bring'
25 'serious appearance'
37-38 'staying up all night hasn't made him pale'
39-40 'hides his worries with a cheerful expression'

ORLÉANS 'Ill will never said well.'
CONSTABLE I will cap that proverb with 'There is flattery in friendship.'   105
ORLÉANS And I will take up that with 'Give the devil his due!'
CONSTABLE Well placed! There stands your friend for the devil. Have at the very eye of that proverb with 'A pox of the devil!'
ORLÉANS You are the better at proverbs by how much 'A fool's bolt is soon shot.'
CONSTABLE You have shot over.   110
ORLÉANS 'Tis not the first time you were overshot.

Enter a Messenger.

MESSENGER My Lord High Constable, the English lie within fifteen hundred paces of your tents.
CONSTABLE Who hath measured the ground?
MESSENGER The Lord Grandpré.   115
CONSTABLE A valiant and most expert gentleman.

Exit Messenger.

Would it were day! Alas, poor Harry of England! He longs not for the dawning as we do.
ORLÉANS What a wretched and peevish fellow is this King of England, to mope with his fat-brained followers so far out of his knowledge.   **[understanding]**
CONSTABLE If the English had any apprehension, they would run away.   120
ORLÉANS That they lack; for if their heads had any intellectual armour, they could never wear such heavy head-pieces.
RAMBURES That island of England breeds very valiant creatures: their mastiffs are of unmatchable courage.   **[blindly]**   125
ORLÉANS Foolish curs, that run winking into the mouth of a Russian bear, and have their heads crushed like rotten apples! You may as well say that's a valiant flea that dare eat his breakfast on the lip of a lion.
CONSTABLE Just, just; and the men do sympathize with the mastiffs in robustious and rough coming on, leaving their wits with their wives. And then, give them great meals of beef, and iron and steel, they will eat like wolves, and fight like devils.   130
ORLÉANS Ay, but these English are shrewdly out of beef.   **[badly]**
CONSTABLE Then shall we find tomorrow they have only stomachs to eat, and none to fight. Now is it time to arm. Come, shall we about it?   135
ORLÉANS It is now two o'clock; but, let me see — by ten We shall have each a hundred Englishmen.

Exeunt.

Left-margin notes:

101-108 Bourbon and Constable are quoting proverbs at each other.
102-3 'Friends tend to flatter each other'
107-8 'You're as fast at quoting proverbs as "A fool is quick to fire his arrow"'
109 'Now you've shot past the target'
110 'It's not the first time someone's shot further than you'

> Hope this one goes further!

118-20 'What a miserable, foolish person this King of England is, wandering aimlessly about with his followers, not knowing what he's doing'
122-3 'if they had any intellectual armour (brains) they wouldn't be able to wear such heavy helmets'
125 Mastiffs are huge, fierce dogs, used by Elizabethans for bear-baiting.
130-32 'True, true; and the men are like the mastiffs, the way they attack so fiercely — they leave their brains to their wives'
135-6 'Tomorrow we'll find they only want to eat, not fight'

Leave me alone!

His liberal eye doth give to every one,
Thawing cold fear, that mean and gentle all
Behold, as may unworthiness define,
A little touch of Harry in the night.
And so our scene must to the battle fly,
Where — oh for pity! — we shall much disgrace,
With four or five most vile and ragged foils
Right ill-disposed in brawl ridiculous,
The name of Agincourt. Yet sit and see,
Minding true things by what their mockeries be.

Exit

ACT 4
SCENE 1

Enter King Henry and Gloucester, meeting Bedford.

KING HENRY Gloucester, 'tis true that we are in great danger;
The greater therefore should our courage be. —
Good morrow, brother Bedford. God Almighty!
There is some soul of goodness in things evil,
Would men observingly distil it out:
For our bad neighbour makes us early stirrers,
Which is both healthful and good husbandry.
Besides, they are our outward consciences,
And preachers to us all, admonishing
That we should dress us fairly for our end.
Thus may we gather honey from the weed
And make a moral of the devil himself.

Enter Erpingham.

Good morrow, old Sir Thomas Erpingham!
A good soft pillow for that good white head
Were better than a churlish turf of France.
ERPINGHAM Not so, my liege, this lodging likes me better,
Since I may say, 'Now lie I like a king.'
KING HENRY 'Tis good for men to love their present pains.
Upon example so the spirit is eased,
And when the mind is quickened, out of doubt
The organs, though defunct and dead before,
Break up their drowsy grave and newly move
With casted slough and fresh legerity.
Lend me thy cloak, Sir Thomas. — Brothers both,
Commend me to the princes in our camp.
Do my good morrow to them, and anon
Desire them all to my pavilion.
GLOUCESTER We shall, my liege.

45

50

5

10

miserable

15

20

nimbleness

25

ERPINGHAM Shall I attend your grace?
KING HENRY   No, my good knight;
Go with my brothers to my lords of England.
I and my bosom must debate a while,
And then I would no other company.
ERPINGHAM The Lord in heaven bless thee, noble Harry!
Exeunt all except King Henry.
KING HENRY God-a-mercy, old heart, thou speak'st cheerfully.

Enter Pistol.

God have mercy

PISTOL *Qui vous là?*
KING HENRY A friend.
PISTOL Discuss unto me, art thou officer, or art thou base,
common and popular?
KING HENRY I am a gentleman of a company.
PISTOL Trail'st thou the puissant pike?
KING HENRY Even so. What are you?
PISTOL As good a gentleman as the Emperor.
KING HENRY Then you are a better than the King.
PISTOL The King's a bawcock and a heart of gold, a lad of life,
an imp of Fame, of parents good, of fist most valiant. I
kiss his dirty shoe, and from heartstring I love the lovely
bully. What is thy name?

fine fellow

KING HENRY Harry le Roy.
PISTOL Le Roy? A Cornish name: art thou of Cornish crew?
KING HENRY No, I am a Welshman.
PISTOL Know'st thou Llewellyn?
KING HENRY Yes.
PISTOL Tell him I'll knock his leek about his pate upon Saint
Davy's day.
KING HENRY Do not you wear your dagger in your cap that
day, lest he knock that about yours.
PISTOL Art thou his friend?
KING HENRY And his kinsman too.
PISTOL The *fico* for thee then!

fig

KING HENRY I thank you. God be with you!
PISTOL My name is Pistol called.
Exit.
KING HENRY It sorts well with your fierceness.

Enter Llewellyn and Gower, from different directions.

GOWER Captain Llewellyn!

30

35

40

45

50

55

60

Margin notes:

45-46 'so that all the nobles, and all the ordinary people experience, within their limits'

52-53 'Sit and watch, picturing the true things in your mind, with the help of our poor version'

This scene's a biggie. Henry meets all sorts of people from his army as he passes round the camp in disguise.

4-5 'there's some sort of goodness to be found in evil, if only men would carefully separate it out'

7 'good housekeeping' i.e. sensible and practical

9-12 'warning us to be well prepared for our deaths. If you try you can even get honey from weeds, and learn a good lesson from the devil himself'

16 'I prefer these lodgings'

19 'by following this example the spirit is eased'

23 'like a snake that's shed its old skin'

25-27 'Give my regards to the English nobles. Tell them "Good morning" from me, and ask them to meet at my tent shortly'

31-2 'I need some time to think things through, and I'd rather be alone'

35 'Who goes there?'

37-8 'Tell me, are you an officer, or an ordinary soldier?'

39 'low-ranking officer'

40 'Do you fight with the mighty pike?' A pike is a combined spear and axe on a pole 3 metres long...nasty.

43 'even nobler'

44 literally 'a lovely chicken'

45 'the son of a famous family'

48 French for 'Harry the King'.

53-54 'Tell him I'll beat him over the head with a leek on St. David's day.'

55-56 'Don't wear that dagger in your cap then — he might use it to beat your head'

BANG!

62 'It suits your fierce nature.'

LLEWELLYN So! In the name of Jesu Christ, speak fewer. It is the greatest admiration in the universal world, when the true and ancient prerogatives and laws of the wars is not kept. If you would take the pains but to examine the wars of Pompey the Great you shall find, I warrant you, that there is no tiddle-taddle nor pibble-pabble in Pompey's camp. I warrant you, you shall find the ceremonies of the wars, and the cares of it, and the forms of it, and the sobriety of it, and the modesty of it to be otherwise.

GOWER Why, the enemy is loud; you hear him all night.

LLEWELLYN If the enemy is an ass and a fool and a prating coxcomb, is it meet, think you, that we should also, look you, be an ass and a fool and a prating coxcomb? In your own conscience now?

GOWER I will speak lower. [more quietly]

LLEWELLYN I pray you and beseech you that you will.

Exeunt Gower and Llewellyn.

KING HENRY Though it appear a little out of fashion, There is much care and valour in this Welshman.

Enter three soldiers — John Bates, Alexander Court, and Michael Williams.

COURT Brother John Bates, is not that the morning which breaks yonder?

BATES I think it be; but we have no great cause to desire the approach of day.

WILLIAMS We see yonder the beginning of the day, but I think we shall never see the end of it — who goes there?

KING HENRY A friend.

WILLIAMS Under what captain serve you?

KING HENRY Under Sir Thomas Erpingham.

WILLIAMS A good old commander and a most kind gentleman. I pray you, what thinks he of our estate?

KING HENRY Even as men wrecked upon a sand, that look to be washed off the next tide.

BATES He has not told his thought to the King?

KING HENRY No, nor is it not meet he should. For though I speak it to you, I think the King is but a man, as I am. The violet smells to him as it doth to me. All his senses have but human conditions. His ceremonies laid by, in his [robes] nakedness he appears but a man; and though his affections are higher mounted than ours, yet when they stoop they [feelings] stoop with the like wing. Therefore when he sees reason of fears as we do, his fears, out of doubt, be of the same

relish as ours are. Yet, in reason, no man should possess him with any appearance of fear, lest he, by showing it, should dishearten his army.

BATES He may show what outward courage he will, but I believe, as cold a night as 'tis, he could wish himself in Thames up to the neck; and so I would he were, and I by him, at all adventures, so we were quit here.

KING HENRY By my troth, I will speak my conscience of the [true feelings] King: I think he would not wish himself anywhere but where he is.

BATES Then I would he were here alone; so should he be sure to be ransomed, and a many poor men's lives saved.

KING HENRY I dare say you love him not so ill to wish him here alone, howsoever you speak this to feel other men's minds. Methinks I could not die anywhere so contented as in the King's company, his cause being just and his quarrel honourable.

WILLIAMS That's more than we know.

BATES Ay, or more than we should seek after, for we know enough if we know we are the King's subjects. If his cause be wrong, our obedience to the King wipes the crime of it out of us.

WILLIAMS But if the cause be not good, the King himself hath a heavy reckoning to make, when all those legs and arms and heads chopped off in a battle, shall join together at the latter day and cry all 'We died at such a place'; some swearing, some crying for a surgeon, some upon their wives left poor behind them, some upon the debts they owe, some upon their children rawly left. I am afeard there are few die well that die in battle, for how can they charitably dispose of anything when blood is their argument? Now if these men do not die well it will be a black matter for the King, that led them to it, who to disobey the King were against all proportion of subjection. [left poor]

KING HENRY So if a son that is by his father sent about [blame] merchandise do sinfully miscarry upon the sea, the imputation of his wickedness, by your rule, should be imposed upon his father that sent him; or if a servant, under his master's command transporting a sum of money, be assailed by robbers and die in many [attacked] irreconciled iniquities, you may call the business of the master the author of the servant's damnation. But this is not so: the King is not bound to answer the particular endings of his soldiers, the father of his son, nor the [plan on] master of his servant; for they purpose not their death when they purpose their services. Besides, there is no

64-6 'it's amazing thing when the old war methods are ignored'

68 A brilliant and popular Roman general.

69 'no foolish chatter'

74-5 'boastful idiot'

Shhhh!

80-81 'This Welshman's got a funny style, but he's careful and brave'

92 'what does he think of our situation'

93-94 'He thinks we're like shipwrecked men, stranded on a sand bank, expecting to be washed off on the next tide'

96 'and it's not right'

98-99 'His feelings are only the normal human ones'

103-4 'his fears must feel the same as ours'

104-6 'In fact, no man should show he is afraid, in case he makes the rest of the army nervous'

110 'come what may, so long as we were finished here'

115 'captured and his ransom payed' That way there wouldn't have to be a battle.

17-18 'even if that's what you say to test other men's opinions'

122 'more than we can hope to know'

123-5 'If he is acting wrongly, we commit no crime by helping him — we're just being obedient'

128-9 'on Judgement Day' Williams is imagining all the hacked up bodies from the battle joing back together at the end of the world.

133-5 'how can people settle their affairs in a generous way, when all their thoughts are of bloodshed'

136-7 'to disobey the King would be against all that is expected of a subject'

139 'die without confessing his sins to a priest' If you didn't confess your sins before you died it was believed you would go to Hell.

143-4 'without confessing his sins'

146-7 'the King doesn't have to answer for the exact way each soldier dies'

Section Nine — The Key Scenes

king, be his cause never so spotless, if it come to the
arbitrament of swords, can try it out with all unspotted 150
soldiers. Some, peradventure, have on them the guilt of
premeditated and contrived murder; some, of beguiling
virgins with the broken seals of perjury; some, making the
wars their bulwark, that have before gored the gentle 155
bosom of peace, with pillage and robbery. Now if these
men have defeated the law and outrun native punishment,
though they can outstrip men, they have no wings to fly
from God. War is His beadle, war is His vengeance; so that
here men are punished for before-breach of the King's 160
laws, in now the King's quarrel. Where they feared the
death they have borne life away, and where they would be
safe they perish. Then if they die unprovided, no more is
the King guilty of their damnation than he was before guilty
of those impieties for the which they are now visited. Every 165
subject's duty is the King's, but every subject's soul is his
own. Therefore should every soldierin the wars do as every
sick man in his bed, wash every mote out of his conscience;
and dying so death is to him advantage; or not dying, the **stain**
time was blessedly lost wherein such preparation was 170
gained; and in him that escapes, it were not sin to think that,
making God so free an offer, he let him outlive that day to
see His greatness and to teach others how they should
prepare.

WILLIAMS 'Tis certain, every man that dies ill, the ill upon his own 175
head; the King is not to answer it.

BATES I do not desire he should answer for me, and yet I
determine to fight lustily for him. **enthusiastically**

KING HENRY I myself heard the King say he would not be 180
ransomed.

WILLIAMS Ay, he said so to make us fight cheerfully; but when our
throats are cut he may be ransomed and we ne'er the wiser.

KING HENRY If I live to see it, I will never trust his word after.

WILLIAMS You pay him then! That's a perilous shot out of an 185
elder-gun that a poor and a private displeasure can do
against a monarch. You may as well go about to turn the
sun to ice, with fanning in his face with a peacock's feather.
You'll never trust his word after! Come, 'tis a foolish saying.

KING HENRY Your reproof is something too round; I should be 190
angry wth you if the time were convenient.

WILLIAMS Let it be a quarrel between us, if you live.

KING HENRY I embrace it.

WILLIAMS How shall I know thee again?

KING HENRY Give me any gage of thine, and I will wear it in my

195 **hat** bonnet. Then if ever thou dar'st acknowledge it I will
make it my quarrel.

WILLIAMS Here's my glove. Give me another of thine.

KING HENRY There.

WILLIAMS This I will also wear in my cap. If ever thou come
200 to me and say after tomorrow 'This is my glove,' by this
hand I will take thee a box on the ear.

KING HENRY If ever I live to see it I will challenge it.

WILLIAMS Thou dar'st as well be hanged.

KING HENRY Well, I will do it, though I take thee in the King's
205 company.

WILLIAMS Keep thy word. Fare thee well.

BATES Be friends, you English fools, be friends! We have
French quarrels enough if you could tell how to reckon.

KING HENRY Indeed, the French may lay twenty French
210 crowns to one they will beat us, for they bear them on
their shoulders; but it is no English treason to cut French
crowns, and tomorrow the King himself will be a clipper.

Exeunt soldiers.

worried
Upon the King! 'Let us our lives, our souls,
215 Our debts, our careful wives,
Our children and our sins lay on the King!
We must bear all. O hard condition,
Twin-born with greatness, subject to the breath
Of every fool whose sense no more can feel
220 **pain** But his own wringing! What infinite heart's ease
Must kings neglect that private men enjoy!
And what have kings that privates have not too,
Save ceremony, save general ceremony?
And what art thou, thou idol ceremony?
225 **false god** What kind of god art thou, that suffer'st more
Of mortal griefs than do thy worshippers?
incomes What are thy rents, what are thy comings-in?
O ceremony, show me but thy worth!
What is thy soul of adoration?
230 Art thou aught else but place, degree and form,
Creating awe and fear in other men,
Wherein thou art less happy, being feared,
Than they in fearing?
What drink'st thou oft, instead of homage sweet,
235 But poison'd flattery? O be sick, great greatness,
And bid thy ceremony give thee cure!
Think'st thou the fiery fever will go out
With titles blown from adulation?
Will it give place to flexure and low bending?

Left margin notes

150-51 'when an issue is resolved by fighting'

154 'broken seals of false promises'

154-5 'using the war as a shield'

159 'officer who gives out punishment'

160-61 'punished for breaking the law in the past, in the King's current quarrel'

163-5 'If they die unprepared, the King's no more guilty of anything they've done than he was before they went to war'

184-5 'a badly aimed shot out of a toy gun'

189 'your criticism is a little too direct'

193 The 'thee' here is a bit too personal — it's meant rudely.

194 'give me one of your possessions as a token of the fight'

Oi, are you starting one?

Right margin notes

197 The glove is the gage Henry's just asked for. A glove was the usual symbol of an agreement to fight.

201 'punch you in the ear'

203 'You might as well hope to be hanged.'

204-5 'even if I find you talking to the King'

209-10 'French coins' or 'French heads'

211-12 'It's no crime in England to cut French crowns'

212 A clipper trimmed pieces from coins till he had enough gold to sell. The punishment was death. Henry'a making a joke about French crowns (coins vs. heads). He means he'll kill lots of Frenchmen tomorrow.

219-20 'Kings must miss out on so much of the relaxation that ordinary people enjoy!'

224-5 'What kind of god are you, when you have to put up with more human pain than your worshippers do?'

228-9 'What's the secret of the adoration people give you? Is there anything more to you than status and appearances?'

236-7 'Do you think the fever of responsibility can be soothed with flattery?'

Section Nine — The Key Scenes

Left margin notes

239-40 'You can make a beggar kneel, but if his knee was broken you couldn't force it to heal'

242 'You can't fool me — I'm a king'

243 'holy oil, royal staff, and ball' These are all used at the crowning of an English king or queen.

252 'with a full stomach, and an untroubled mind'

255 'footman who follows a carriage'

256 'works under the gaze of Phoebus.' Phoebus was the Greek sun god, said to ride his chariot across the sky every day.

261-3 'if it wasn't for ceremony, the poor man, who works all day and sleeps all night, would have every advantage over a king'

265-7 'in his simple mind, he little knows what effort the king makes to keep the peace, which the peasant is best able to enjoy'

274 'the ability to count'

276-8 'don't think about the bad things my dad did when he took the crown from Richard II. I've had his body reburied'

Oh, yeah, like being a peasant's so great.

Main text

240
Canst thou, when thou command'st the beggar's knee,
Command the health of it? No, thou proud dream
That play'st so subtly with a king's repose,
I am a king that find thee, and I know
'Tis not the balm, the sceptre and the ball, — **staff**
The sword, the mace, the crown imperial,
245
The intertissued robe of gold and pearl, — **woven**
The farcèd title running 'fore the king, — **richly stuffed (like meat)**
The throne he sits on, nor the tide of pomp
That beats upon the high shore of this world —
No, not all these, thrice-gorgeous ceremony,
250
Not all these, laid in bed majestical,
Can sleep so soundly as the wretched slave,
Who with a body filled and vacant mind
Gets him to rest, crammed with distressful bread; — **hard-earned**
Never sees horrid night, the child of hell,
255
But like a lackey from the rise to set,
Sweats in the eye of Phoebus, and all night
Sleeps in Elysium; next day after dawn — **heaven**
Doth rise and help Hyperion to his horse; — **Phoebus' dad**
And follows so the ever-running year
260
With profitable labour to his grave.
And but for ceremony such a wretch,
Winding up days with toil and nights with sleep,
Had the fore-hand and vantage of a king.
The slave, a member of the country's peace,
265
Enjoys it; but in gross brain little wots
What watch the king keeps to maintain the peace,
Whose hours the peasant best advantages.

Enter Erpingham.

ERPINGHAM My lord, your nobles, jealous of your absence, — **worried about**
Seek you through your camp to find you.
270
KING HENRY   Good old knight,
Collect them all together at my tent.
I'll be before thee.
ERPINGHAM   I shall do't my lord.

Exit. King Henry kneels.

KING HENRY O God of battles, steel my soldiers' hearts; — **strengthen**
Possess them not with fears. Take from them now
275
The sense of reckoning ere th'opposèd numbers
Pluck their hearts from them. Not today, O Lord,
O not today, think not upon the fault
My father made in compassing the crown.
I Richard's body have interrèd new,
280
And on it have bestowed more contrite tears — **regretful**
Than from it issued forcèd drops of blood.

Five hundred poor I have in yearly pay,
Who twice a day their withered hands hold up
Toward heaven to pardon blood; and I have built
285 **chapels** Two chantries, where the sad and solemn priests
Sing still for Richard's soul. More will I do,
Though all that I can do is nothing worth,
Since that my penitence comes after all,
Imploring pardon.
GLOUCESTER (*within*) My liege!
KING HENRY   My brother Gloucester's voice?

Enter Gloucester.

I know thy errand, I will go with thee.
290
The day, my friends and all things stay for me.

Exeunt.

ACT 4
SCENE 2

Enter Bourbon, Orléans, Rambures and Beaumont.

ORLÉANS The sun doth gild our armour: up, my lords!
BOURBON *Montez à cheval!* My horse, *varlet laquais;* ha!
ORLÉANS O brave spirit!
BOURBON *Via les eaux et terres!*
5 ORLÉANS *Rien puis? L'air et feu!*
BOURBON *Cieux,* cousin Orléans!

Enter the Constable.

                              Now, my Lord Constable!
CONSTABLE Hark how our steeds for present service neigh!
BOURBON Mount them and make incision in their hides,
That their hot blood may spin in English eyes
10 And dout them with superfluous courage, ha!
RAMBURES What, will you have them weep our horses' blood?
How shall we then behold their natural tears?

Enter a Messenger

MESSENGER The English are embattled, you French peers.
CONSTABLE To horse, you gallant princes, straight to horse!
15 Do but behold yon poor and starvèd band,
And your fair show shall suck away their souls,
short chopping sword Leaving them but the shales and husks of men.
There is not work enough for all our hands,
Scarce blood enough in all their sickly veins
20 To give each naked curtle-axe a stain

Right margin notes

281-3 'I pay five hundred poor people a pension, so they'll pray for pardon'

287-8 'seeing as my apology comes after the bad deeds, in the hope of pardon'

It's the morning and the French nobles are ready for battle. The Constable and Grandpré both report that the English army looks feeble, and easy to beat.

2 'Get on your horses! Fetch my horse, servant!'

4 'Cut through water and land!' The water and land are heavy elements which would drag the horse down.

5 'What, no air or fire?'

6 'The heavens,' cousin Orléans!'

7 'Listen to our horses, neighing for immediate action!'

9 'dot them with extra courage'

13 'drawn up in lines for battle'

15-16 'you'll only have to look at that poor, starving bunch, and the very look of you will suck away their souls'

That our French gallants shall today draw out
And sheathe for lack of sport. Let us but blow on them,
The vapour of our valour will o'erturn them.
'Tis positive 'gainst all exceptions, lords,
That our superfluous lackeys, and our peasants,
Who in unnecessary action swarm
About our squares of battle, were enough
To purge this field of such a hilding foe, **worthless**
Though we upon this mountain's basis by
Took stand for idle speculation:
But that our honours must not. What's to say?
A very little little let us do,
And all is done. Then let the trumpets sound
The tucket sonance and the note to mount,
For our approach shall so much dare the field **intimidate**
That England shall couch down in fear and yield.

Enter Grandpré

GRANDPRE Why do you stay so long, my lords of France?
Yon island carrions, desperate of their bones,
Ill-favouredly become the morning field.
Their ragged curtains poorly are let loose, **battle flags**
And our air shakes them passing scornfully.
Big Mars seems bankrupt in their beggared host
And faintly through a rusty beaver peeps.
The horsemen sit like fixèd candlesticks,
With torch-staves in their hand, and their poor jades **nags**
Lob down their heads, dropping the hides and hips,
The gum down-roping from their pale-dead eyes,
And in their pale dull mouths the gemmeled bit **jointed**
Lies foul with chewed grass, still and motionless.
And their executors, the knavish crows,
Fly o'er them all, impatient for their hour.
Description cannot suit itself in words
To demonstrate the life of such a battle
In life so lifeless as it shows itself. **wait**
CONSTABLE They have said their prayers, and they stay for death.
BOURBON Shall we go send them dinners, and fresh suits,
And give their fasting horses provender, **a feed**
And after fight with them?
CONSTABLE I stay but for my guidon. To the field!
I will the banner from a trumpet take,
And use it for my haste. Come, come away!
The sun is high, and we outwear the day.

Exeunt.

23 **'the very breath of our bravery will knock them down'**
24-5 **'I guarantee you, my lords — our spare servants and our peasants'**
29-30 **'even if we went off and watched from the foot of that mountain, doing nothing'**
34 **Commands played on a trumpet, to tell soldiers to march, and get on horses.**
38-9 **'those lumps of meat from the island, who don't seem to care if they lose their bones, are a blot on the morning field'**
42-3 **'That worn out army makes Mars, the god of war, look powerless. He just peeps out through a rusty helmet'**
46-7 **'hang their heads, their skin and hips sag, and gum runs down in strings from their deathly pale eyes'**
50 **Usually the black-robed lawyers who sort out a will, but here, the crows who will pick the soldiers bones.**
52-54 **'There aren't words to prove that such a lifeless army lives'**
59 **'I'm just waiting for my battle standard.' A battle standard showed a noble's coat of arms. The noble's followers could find out where they were meant to be in the battle by looking for the standard.**

ACT 4
SCENE 3

The English are nervous. Henry makes a speech which gives them all courage. Montjoy asks Henry to give up while he can. Henry sends him away, and the English set out for battle.

Enter Gloucester, Bedford, Exeter, Erpingham with all his host, Salisbury and Westmorland.

GLOUCESTER Where is the King?
BEDFORD The King himself is rode to view their battle.
WESTMORLAND Of fighting men they have full threescore thousand.
EXETER There's five to one; besides they are all fresh.
SALISBURY God's arm strike with us! 'Tis a fearful odds.
command post God be wi' you, princes all; I'll to my charge.
If we no more meet till we meet in heaven,
Then joyfully, my noble lord of Bedford,
My dear Lord Gloucester, and my good lord Exeter,
And my kind kinsman, warriors all, adieu.
BEDFORD Farewell, good Salisbury, and good luck go with thee.
EXETER Farewell, kind lord. Fight valiantly today.
remind And yet I do thee wrong to mind thee of it,
For thou art framed of the firm truth of valour.

Exit Salisbury.

BEDFORD He is as full of valour as of kindness,
Princely in both.

Enter King Henry.

WESTMORLAND O that we now had here
But one ten thousand of those men in England
That do no work today!
KING HENRY What's he that wishes so?
My cousin Westmorland? No, my fair cousin.
If we are marked to die, we are enough
To do our country loss, and if to live,
The fewer men, the greater share of honour.
greedy God's will, I pray thee wish not one man more.
By Jove, I am not covetous for gold,
Nor care I who doth feed upon my cost;
upsets It earns me not if men my garments wear;
Such outward things dwell not in my desires.
But if it be a sin to covet honour,
I am the most offending soul alive.
No, faith, my coz, wish not a man from England.
cousin God's peace, I would not lose so great an honour
As one man more, methinks, would share from me,
For the best hope I have. O do not wish one more!
Rather proclaim it Westmorland, through my host,

2 **'The King's ridden out to see their army'**
3 **'60,000'**
7 **'even if we don't see each other again till we're in heaven'**

14 **'you're built out of the firm truth of courage'**
20-22 **'If we are chosen to die, there's enough of us for our country to feel the loss. If we are chosen to live, then the fewer there are of us, the bigger our share of the glory'**
25 **'at my expense'**
30 **'don't wish for the help of a single man'**
31-3 **'I wouldn't want to lose any more honour than one man would take from me, even if it was in exchange for my best hope'**
34 **'announce it all through the army'**

Left margin annotations

35-9 'anyone who doesn't feel up to fighting can go; he'll get a passport and travel money. I wouldn't want to die with anyone who was reluctant to die with me'

40 Crispin and Crispian were two brothers who became the patron saints of shoemakers. St. Crispin's day is October 25.

44 'live to see old age'

47 'roll up his sleeve'

49-51 'everything gets forgotten, but this old boy will remember (with a few improvements to the story) what he did that day'

57 'St. Crispin's Day'

61-3 'Whoever spills his blood today alongside me, will become my brother; no matter how lowly he may be, today will make him more of a gentleman'

66 'feel ashamed of themselves'

68-70 'take your position quickly. The French are handsomely drawn up in their lines, and will charge us very soon'

72 'Death to anyone who isn't eager now!'

76-7 'now you've wished we had 5,000 men less, which I like better than wishing we had one more'

Play text (lines 35–75)

35
That he which hath no stomach to this fight,
Let him depart; his passport shall be made
And crowns for convoy put into his purse.
We would not die in that man's company
That fears his fellowship to die with us.

40
This day is called the Feast of Crispian:
He that outlives this day and comes safe home
Will stand a-tiptoe when this day is named
And rouse him at the name of Crispian.
He that shall see this day and live old age,

45 *(night before)*
Will yearly on the vigil feast his neighbours,
And say 'Tomorrow is Saint Crispian.'
Then will he strip his sleeve and show his scars,
And say 'These wounds I had on Crispin's day.'
Old men forget; yet all shall be forgot,

50
But he'll remember, with advantages,
What feats he did that day. Then shall our names,
Familiar in his mouth as household words,
Harry the king, Bedford and Exeter,
Warwick and Talbot, Salisbury and Gloucester,

55
Be in their flowing cups freshly remembered.
This story shall the good man teach his son,
And Crispin Crispian shall ne'er go by
From this day to the ending of the world,
But we in it shall be remembered —

60
We few, we happy few, we band of brothers;
For he today that sheds his blood with me
Shall be my brother; be he ne'er so vile,
This day shall gentle his condition.
And gentlemen in England now abed

65
Shall think themselves accursed they were not here,
And hold their manhoods cheap, whiles any speaks
That fought with us upon Saint Crispin's day.

Enter Salisbury.

70
SALISBURY My sovereign lord, bestow yourself with speed.
The French are bravely in their battles set
And will with all expedience charge on us.

KING HENRY All things are ready, if our minds be so.

WESTMORLAND Perish the man whose mind is backward now!

KING HENRY Thou dost not wish more help from England, coz?

75
WESTMORLAND God's will, my liege, would you and I alone,
Without more help, could fight this royal battle!

KING HENRY Why, now thou hast unwished five thousand men,
Which likes me better than to wish us one.
You know your places. God be with you all!

Tucket. Enter Mountjoy.

Play text (lines 80–120)

80
MOUNTJOY Once more I come to know of thee, King Harry,
If for thy ransom thou wilt now compound,
Before thy most assured overthrow:

whirlpool
For certainly thou art so near the gulf
Thou needs must be englutted. Besides, in mercy,

85
The Constable desires thee thou wilt mind
Thy followers of repentance, that their souls
May make a peaceful and a sweet retire
From off these fields where, wretches, their poor bodies
Must lie and fester.

KING HENRY   Who hath sent thee now?

MONTJOY The Constable of France.

90
KING HENRY I pray thee bear my former answer back:
Bid them achieve me, and then sell my bones.
Good God, why should they mock poor fellows thus?
The man that once did sell the lion's skin
While the beast lived, was killed with hunting him.

95
A many of our bodies shall no doubt
Find native graves, upon the which, I trust,
Shall witness live in brass of this day's work.
And those that leave their valiant bones in France,
Dying like men, though buried in your dunghills,

100
They shall be famed, for there the sun shall greet them,
And draw their honours reeking up to heaven,
Leaving their earthly parts to choke your clime,
The smell whereof shall breed a plague in France.

cracking up
Mark then abounding valour in our English,

105
That being dead, like to the bullets crazing,
Break out into a second course of mischief,
Killing in relapse of mortality.
Let me speak proudly: tell the Constable
We are but warriors for the working day;

110
Our gayness and our gilt are all besmirched
With rainy marching in the painful field.

untidiness
There's not a piece of feather in our host —
Good argument, I hope, we will not fly —

in fine form
115
And time hath worn us into slovenry.
But, by the mass, our hearts are in the trim,
And my poor soldiers tell me yet ere night

before
They'll be in fresher robes, or they will pluck
The gay new coats o'er the French soldiers' heads
And turn them out of service. If they do this,

raised
120
As, if God please, they shall, my ransom then
Will soon be levied. Herald, save thou thy labour:
Come thou no more for ransom, gentle Herald.
They shall have none, I swear, but these my joints,
Which if they have as I will leave 'em them

Right margin annotations

80-1 'whether you'll discuss your ransom, before your certain defeat'

83 'it's impossible for you to escape being sucked in'

84-8 'The Constable asks you to remind your followers to repent their sins, so that their souls will pass away in peace, from these fields where their bodies will lie rotting'

91 'Tell them to capture me and then sell my bones'

95-7 'Many of us will survive today to be buried in English graves, on which today's acts be recorded'

101-3 'draw their honour to heaven, leaving their physical remains to choke your air, and the stink will start a plague in France'

105-7 'when they're dead, like cannon balls shattering, they cause trouble all over again, killing even when they've physically collapsed'

109-10 'we're not exactly in our Sunday best — our bright colours and our gold are muddy'

113-14 'there isn't one feathered plume in the whole army — which proves, I hope, we won't fly away'

117-19 'they'll snatch the bright new coats over the French soldier's heads, and (by taking off their uniform) throw them out of the army'

123-5 'they'll get no ransom except the joints of my body, and the way I plan to leave

Left column (ACT 4 SCENE 6)

127 'you'll never hear a message from me again'

That's it, I'm off.

132 'give the victory to whichever side you want to, God'

> The English are doing well in the battle, but they're not safe yet. When the French make a fresh attack, Henry orders the English to kill all the French prisoners-of-war.

2 'the French are still on the battlefield'

3 'sends greetings'

6 'He was covered in blood from head to toe'

8 'enriching the field with his blood'

9 'companion to his honourable wounds'

11 'wounded all over'

12 'soaked in blood'

17 'fly alongside me'

19 'we stuck together bravely on the battlefield'

27 'a memorial to his love for Suffolk, which ended in a noble death'

---

125   Shall yield them little. Tell the Constable.
MONTJOY I shall, King Harry. And so fare thee well:
   Thou never shalt hear herald any more.

Exit.

KING HENRY I fear thou wilt once more come again for a ransom.

Enter York.

130 YORK My lord, most humbly on my knee I beg
   The leading of the vanguard.   *[first rows of battle]*
KING HENRY Take it, brave York. – Now soldiers, march away,
132   And how thou pleasest, God, dispose the day!

Exeunt.

ACT 4 SCENE 6

Alarum. Enter the King and his train, with prisoners.

KING HENRY Well have we done, thrice-valiant countrymen,
   But all's not done, yet keep the French the field.   *[three times]*
EXETER The Duke of York commends him to your majesty.
KING HENRY Lives he, good uncle? Thrice within this hour
5   I saw him down, thrice up again, and fighting.
   From helmet to the spur all blood he was.
EXETER In which array, brave soldier, doth he lie,   *[state]*
   Larding the plain; and by his bloody side,
   Yoke-fellow to his honour-owing wounds,
10   The noble Earl of Suffolk also lies.
   Suffolk first died, and York, all haggled over,
   Comes to him, where in gore he lay insteeped,
   And takes him by the beard, kisses the gashes   *[wounds]*
   That bloodily did yawn upon his face.
   He cries aloud, 'Tarry, my cousin Suffolk!   *[wait]* 15
15   My soul shall thine keep company to heaven.
   Tarry, sweet soul, for mine, then fly abreast,   *[fought]*
   As in this glorious and well-foughten field
   We kept together in our chivalry.'
   Upon these words I came and cheered him up;
20   He smiled me in the face, raught me his hand,   *[reached]*
   And with a feeble grip, says, 'Dear my lord,
   Commend my service to my sovereign.'
   So did he turn, and over Suffolk's neck
   He threw his wounded arm, and kissed his lips,
25   And so espoused to death, with blood he sealed   *[married]*
   A testament of noble-ending love.
   The pretty and sweet manner of it forced

Right column (ACT 4 SCENE 6 cont. / SCENE 7)

30-32 'but I wasn't man enough, and all my mother's influence flooded through my eyes, and made me burst into tears'

33-4 'I have to come to terms with my flooding eyes, or they will overflow'

35 'Listen, what's this new battle signal?'

> Llewellyn praises Henry. Montjoy announces that the French give up. Henry gives Llewellyn his glove so he can get out of the fight with Williams.

1 'poys' - boys

2-4 'Isn't it as rotten a piece of mischief, as you'll ever find, in your honest opinion now?'

8-10 'because of this the King has ordered every soldier to cut his prisoner's throat'

12 'Big' - great

14 Alexander the Great was one of the most successful generals ever.

17-18 'they're all the same — it's just a little change in the words'

20 'I believe'

23-5 'if you compare Macedon and Monmouth you'll find their locations are very similar'

   Those waters from me which I would have stopped,
   But I had not so much of man in me,
30   And all my mother came into mine eyes   *[tears]*
   And gave me up to tears.
KING HENRY   I blame you not,
   For, hearing this, I must perforce compound
   With my full eyes, or they will issue too.

Alarum.

35   But hark, what new alarum is this same?
   The French have reinforced their scattered men.
   Then every soldier kill his prisoners!
   Give the word through.

Exeunt.

ACT 4 SCENE 7

Enter Llewellyn and Gower.

LLEWELLYN Kill the poys and the luggage! 'Tis expressly against the law of arms. 'Tis as arrant a piece of knavery, mark you now, as can be offert, in your conscience now, is it not?   *[it's]*

5 GOWER 'Tis certain there's not a boy left alive, and the cowardly rascals that ran from the battle ha' done this slaughter. Besides, they have burned and carried away all that was in the King's tent, wherefore the King most worthily hath caused every soldier to cut his prisoner's throat. O, 'tis a gallant king!   *[have]*

10 LLEWELLYN Ay, he was porn at Monmouth, Captain Gower. What call you the town's name where Alexander the Pig was born?   *[excellent]*

GOWER Alexander the Great.

15 LLEWELLYN Why, I pray you, is not 'pig' great? The pig, or the great, or the mighty, or the huge, or the magnanimous, are all one reckonings, save the phrase is a little variations.

20 GOWER I think Alexander the Great was born in Macedon; his father was called Philip of Macedon, as I take it.

LLEWELLYN I think it is in Macedon where Alexander is porn. I tell you, Captain, if you look in the maps of the world, I warrant you shall find, in the comparisons between Macedon and Monmouth, that the situations, look you, is both alike. There is a river in Macedon, and there is also 25 moreover a river at Monmouth. It is called Wye at   *[guarantee]*

Monmouth, but it is out of my prains what is the name of the other river; but 'tis all one, 'tis alike as my fingers is to my fingers, and there is salmons in both. If you mark Alexander's life well, Harry of Monmouth's life is come after it indifferent well, for there is figures in all things.

30 *Alexander, God knows and you know, in his rages, and his furies, and his wraths, and his cholers, and his moods, and his displeasures, and his indignations, and also being a little intoxicate in his prains, did in his ales and his angers, look you, kill his best friend Cleitus.*

35 GOWER *Our king is not like him in that: he never killed any of his friends.*

LLEWELLYN *It is not well done, mark you now, to take the tales*

40 *out of my mouth, ere it is made an end and finished. I speak but in the figures and comparisons of it. As Alexander killed his friend Cleitus, being in his ales and his cups, so also Harry Monmouth, being in his right wits and his good*

45 *judgements, turned away the fat knight with the great-belly doublet: he was full of jests, and gipes, and knaveries, and mocks — I have forgot his name.*

GOWER *Sir John Falstaff.*

LLEWELLYN *That is he. I'll tell you, there is good men porn at Monmouth.*

50 GOWER *Here comes his majesty.*

Alarum. Enter King Henry with Warwick, Gloucester, Exeter, and Bourbon and other prisoners. Flourish.

KING HENRY *I was not angry since I came to France Until this instant. Take a trumpet, herald; Ride thou unto the horsemen on yon hill.*

55 *If they will fight with us bid them come down Or void the field: they do offend our sight. If they'll do neither, we will come to them, And make them skirr away as swift as stones Enforced from the old Assyrian slings.*

60 *Besides, we'll cut the throats of those we have, And not a man of them that we shall take Shall taste our mercy. Go and tell them so.*

Enter Montjoy.

EXETER *Here comes the Herald of the French, my liege.*

GLOUCESTER *His eyes are humbler than they used to be.*

65 KING HENRY *How now, what means this, herald? Know'st thou not That I have fined these bones of mine for ransom? Com'st thou again for ransom?*

MONTJOY *No, great King;*

---

permission
I come to thee for charitable licence, That we may wander o'er this bloody field To book our dead, and then to bury them,

list **70** *To sort our nobles from our common men. For many of our princes — woe the while! — Lie drowned and soaked in mercenary blood; So do our vulgar drench their peasant limbs In blood of princes, and their wounded steeds*

75 *Fret fetlock-deep in gore, and with wild rage Yerk out their armèd heels at their dead masters, Killing them twice. O, give us leave, great King, To view the field in safety and dispose Of their dead bodies!*

permission

80 KING HENRY *I tell thee truly, herald, I know not if the day be ours or no;*

appear *For yet a many of your horsemen peer And gallop o'er the field.*

MONTJOY *The day is yours.*

KING HENRY *Praised be God, and not our strength, for it!*

85 *What is this castle called that stands hard by?*

MONTJOY *They call it Agincourt.*

KING HENRY *Then call we this the field of Agincourt, Fought on the day of Crispin Crispianus.*

LLEWELLYN *Your grandfather of famous memory, an't please*

history books **90** *your majesty, and your great-uncle Edward the Plack Prince of Wales, as I have read in the chronicles, fought a most prave pattle here in France.*

KING HENRY *They did, Llewellyn.*

LLEWELLYN *Your majesty says very true. If your majesty is*

95 *remembered of it, the Welshmen did good service in a garden where leeks did grow, wearing leeks in their Monmouth caps, which your majesty know to this hour is an honourable badge of the service; and I do believe your majesty takes no scorn to wear the leek upon Saint Tavy's day.*

100 KING HENRY *I wear it for a memorable honour, For I am Welsh, you know, good countryman.*

LLEWELLYN *All the water in Wye cannot wash your majesty's Welsh plood out of your pody, I can tell you that. God pless it and preserve it, as long as it pleases His grace, and His majesty too!*

105 KING HENRY *Thanks, good my countryman.*

LLEWELLYN *By Cheshu, I am your majesty's countryman, I care not who know it. I will confess it to all the woreld. I need not to be ashamed of your majesty, praised be God, so long as your majesty is an honest man.*

Top margin notes:

72 Mercenaries are the paid, ordinary soldiers, unlike the nobles.

75-6 'stamp uneasily, ankle deep in blood, and in a fury, lash out with their iron shoes'

78-9 'properly deal with'

80 'I don't know if we've won or not'

82 'You've won'

84 'nearby'

88-90 Henry's great-grandfather was Edward III. His son, Henry's great-uncle, was known as Edward the Black Prince.

90-91 The Battle of Crécy, 1346

94 'fought a brave battle'

95 'tall caps, with no brim, made at Monmouth'

97-8 'I believe your majesty is not ashamed to wear the leek on St. David's day'

106 'Jesus'

Welsh and proud!

Bottom margin notes:

27 'I can't remember'

29-31 'If you look carefully at Alexander's life, you'll see Henry's matches it fairly well, for there are comparisons in all things'

35 'when he was drunk and angry'

36 Alexander killed his best friend at a banquet.

39-41 'Don't interrupt — I'm saying it's similar, not exactly the same'

41-4 'Alexander killed Cleitus when he was drunk: Henry turned away the fat knight when he was sober, and in control of himself'

Fight or run away, it's your choice.

54-5 'if they're going to fight us tell them to come on and do it, or otherwise get off the battlefield'

57-8 'make them run away as fast as stones fired from the old Assyrian slings' Assyria was an ancient kingdom to the East of the Mediterranean.

60-61 'not one of the prisoners we take from now on will be spared'

64-5 'Don't you know I've promised these bones of mine for ransom?'

Section Nine — The Key Scenes

148-9 'If you meet anyone wearing a glove like this, arrest him, if you love me'

151-3 'I would love to see any man on two legs get in trouble over this glove'

You'll like this...

163 'according to the agreement I made'

169-70 'if he loses his temper, he explodes, and is quick to pay back an insult'

The trick Henry has played on Williams is revealed, and Henry makes it up to Williams with a present. The heralds announce the numbers of the French and English dead. The English have done amazingly well.

3-5 'I think you might be in for better luck than you've ever dreamt of'

8 Don't forget — Williams thinks Llewellyn's the man he had an argument with last night.

---

110 KING HENRY God keep me so!

Enter Williams.

Our heralds go with him.
Bring me just notice of the numbers dead
On both our parts.

Exeunt Heralds with Montjoy.

Call yonder fellow hither.

EXETER Soldier, you must come to the King.

115 KING HENRY Soldier, why wear'st thou that glove in thy cap?

WILLIAMS An't please your majesty, 'tis the gage of one that I should fight withal, if he be alive.

KING HENRY An Englishman?

120 WILLIAMS An't please your majesty, a rascal that swaggered with me last night, who, if'a live and ever dare to challenge this glove, I have sworn to take him a box o'th'ear; or if I can see my glove in his cap, which he swore as he was a soldier he would wear if'a lived, I will strike it out soundly.

125 KING HENRY What think you, Captain Llewellyn, is it fit this soldier keep his oath?

LLEWELLYN He is a craven and a villain else, an't please your majesty, in my conscience.

KING HENRY It may be his enemy is a gentleman of great sort, quite from the answer of his degree.

130 LLEWELLYN Though he be as good a gentleman as the devil is, as Lucifer and Belzebub himself, it is necessary, look your grace, that he keep his vow and his oath. If he be perjured, see you now, his reputation is as arrant a villain and a Jack-sauce as ever his black shoe trod upon God's ground and 135 His earth, in my conscience, law.

rude man

KING HENRY Then keep thy vow, sirrah, when thou meet'st the fellow.

WILLIAMS So I will, my liege, as I live.

KING HENRY Who serv'st thou under?

WILLIAMS Under Captain Gower, my liege.

140 LLEWELLYN Gower is a good captain, and is good knowledge and literature in the wars.

KING HENRY Call him hither to me, soldier.

WILLIAMS I will, my liege.

Exit.

KING HENRY Here, Llewellyn, wear thou this favour for me, and 145 stick it in thy cap. When Alençon and myself were down together, I plucked this glove from his helm. If any man challenge this, he is a friend to Alençon, and an enemy to our person. If thou encounter any such, apprehend him, an thou dost me love.

150 LLEWELLYN Your grace does me as great honours as can be desired in the hearts of his subjects. I would fain see the man that has but two legs that shall find himself aggrieved at this glove, that is all: but I would fain see it once, an't please God of His grace that I might.

155 KING HENRY Know'st thou Gower?

LLEWELLYN He is my dear friend, an 't please you.

KING HENRY Pray thee go seek him, and bring him to my tent.

LLEWELLYN I will fetch him.

Exit.

160 KING HENRY My Lord of Warwick, and my brother Gloucester,
Follow Llewellyn closely at the heels.
The glove which I have given him for a favour
May haply purchase him a box o'th'ear;
It is the soldier's. I by bargain should
Wear it myself. Follow, good cousin Warwick.
165 If that the soldier strike him, as I judge
By his blunt bearing he will keep his word,
Some sudden mischief may arise of it,
For I do know Llewellyn valiant,
And, touched with choler, hot as gunpowder,
170 And quickly will return an injury.
Follow, and see there be no harm between them. —
Go you with me, uncle of Exeter.

Exeunt.

ACT 4
SCENE 8

Enter Gower and Williams.

WILLIAMS I warrant it is to knight you, Captain.

guarantee

Enter Llewellyn.

LLEWELLYN God's will and His pleasure, Captain, I beseech you now, come apace to the King. There is more good toward you, peradventure, than is in your knowledge to dream of.

quickly

5 WILLIAMS Sir, know you this glove?

LLEWELLYN Know the glove? I know the glove is a glove.

WILLIAMS I know this; and thus I challenge it.

He strikes him.

---

112 'an exact record'

'Scuse me, mate, but there's a glove on your head...

116-17 'It's a token given me by someone to show we'll fight, if he's still alive'

119-20 'was throwing his weight around with me'

120-23 'if he's alive and dares to challenge this glove I've sworn to punch him in the ear; or if I see him wearing my glove in his hat, which he swore he would, I'll knock it out'

126-7 'If he doesn't stick to his oath he's a worthless rat, in my opinion'

128-9 'a very grand gentleman, too noble to answer a challenge from his sort'

132 'proved a liar'

136 Like saying 'sir' but to someone less important than you.

140-41 'he's well read'

144 He means the glove. It's a badge of honour now, instead of a promise to fight.

145-6 'fighting, I took it from his helmet'

48-50 'I beg you to look on what happened when you were in disguise as your fault, not mine'

56 'you had better'

57-8 'he's brave enough'

One Shilling

64-5 'what reason have you got to be so shy'

69 'noble prisoners'

Fiddlesticks.

76 'nobles carrying banners showing their coat of arms'

80 'given the title of knight'

LLEWELLYN God's blood, an arrant traitor as any's in the universal world, or in France, or in England!

GOWER How now, sir? You villain!

WILLIAMS Do you think I'll be forsworn?

LLEWELLYN Stand away Captain Gower: I will give treason his payment into plows, I warrant you.

denied

WILLIAMS I am no traitor.

LLEWELLYN That's a lie in thy throat. I charge you in his majesty's name, apprehend him: he's a friend of the Duke Alençon's.

arrest

Enter Warwick and Gloucester.

WARWICK How now, how now, what's the matter?

LLEWELLYN My Lord of Warwick, here is, praised be God for it, a most contagious treason come to light, look you, as you shall desire in a summer's day. Here is his majesty.

Enter the King and Exeter.

KING HENRY How now! what's the matter?

LLEWELLYN My liege, here is a villain and a traitor, that, look your grace, has struck the glove which your majesty is take out of the helmet of Alençon.

WILLIAMS My liege, this was my glove, here is the fellow of it; and he that I gave it to in change promised to wear it in his cap. I promised to strike him if he did. I met this man with my glove in his cap, and I have been as good as my word.

LLEWELLYN Your majesty, hear now, saving your majesty's manhood, what an arrant, rascally, beggarly, lousy knave it is. I hope your majesty is pear me testimony, and witness, and avouchment, that this is the glove of Alençon that your majesty is give me, in your conscience, now.

KING HENRY Give me thy glove, soldier. Look, here is the fellow of it.
'Twas I indeed thou promised to strike,
And thou hast given me most bitter terms.

LLEWELLYN An't please your majesty, let his neck answer for it, if there is any martial law in the world.

KING HENRY How canst thou make me satisfaction?

WILLIAMS All offences, my lord, come from the heart: never came any from mine that might offend your majesty.

KING HENRY It was ourself thou didst abuse.

WILLIAMS Your majesty came not like yourself: you appeared to me but as a common man — witness the night, your garments, your lowliness; and what your highness suffered

10

15

20

25

30

35

40

45

under that shape, I beseech you take it for your own fault, and not mine; for had you been as I took you for, I made no offence: therefore, I beseech your highness, pardon me.

KING HENRY Here, uncle Exeter, fill this glove with crowns,

coins

And give it to this fellow. Keep it, fellow,
And wear it for an honour in thy cap
Till I do challenge it. Give him the crowns.
And, Captain, you must needs be friends with him.

LLEWELLYN By this day and this light, the fellow has mettle enough in his belly. Hold, there is twelve pence for you, and I pray you to serve God, and keep you out of prawls, and prabbles, and quarrels, and dissensions, and I warrant you it is the better for you.

WILLIAMS I will none of your money.

LLEWELLYN It is with a good will: I can tell you, it will serve you to mend your shoes. Come, wherefore should you be so pashful? Your shoes is not so good. 'Tis a good shilling, I warrant you, or I will change it.

Enter an English Herald.

KING HENRY Now, herald, are the dead numbered?

HERALD Here is the number of the slaughtered French.

He gives him a paper.

KING HENRY What prisoners of good sort are taken, uncle?

EXETER Charles, Duke of Orléans, nephew to the king; John, Duke of Bourbon, and Lord Boucicault; Of other lords and barons, knights and squires, Full fifteen hundred, besides common men.

KING HENRY This note doth tell me of ten thousand French That in the field lie slain. Of princes, in this number, And nobles bearing banners, there lie dead One hundred twenty-six: added to these, Of knights, esquires, and gallant gentlemen, Eight thousand and four hundred; of the which, Five hundred were but yesterday dubbed knights. So that in these ten thousand they have lost, There are but sixteen hundred mercenaries; The rest are princes, barons, lords, knights, squires And gentlemen of blood and quality. The names of those their nobles that lie dead: Charles Delabret, High Constable of France; Jacques of Chatillón, Admiral of France; The Master of the Crossbows, Lord Rambures; Great Master of France, the brave Sir Guiscard Dauphin; John Duke of Alençon; Anthony Duke of Brabant, The brother to the Duke of Burgundy;

50

55

60

65

70

75

80

85

90

13-14 'I'll make him pay for his treason with blows'

Get him!

20-22 'as disgusting a treason has been revealed as you may care to imagine'

28 'swapped it with'

33-5 'I hope your majesty will back me up in saying this is Alençon's glove, which you gave me'

36-9 'here's the matching glove. It was really me you promised to fight, and you've insulted me bitterly'

40 'let him hang for it'

42 'How are you going to make it up to me?'

45 'It was me you were rude to.'

46 'you were in disguise'

Section Nine — The Key Scenes

The author's done his best to tell this whopping great story. Henry's achievements were magnificent, but he died young. His baby son became King, and everything was lost.

2 'our humble author has followed the story, squeezing mighty men into a little space'

4 'spoiling their full glory, by telling the story in little snippets'

5-6 'Henry lived a very short time, but he lived magnificently'

7 France

9-12 'Henry the Sixth was crowned King of England and France when he was still a baby in swaddling clothes. So many people had a hand in helping him run his country, that France was lost, and England suffered'

EPILOGUE

Enter Chorus

CHORUS Thus far, with rough and all-unable pen,
Our bending author hath pursued the story,
In little room confining mighty men,
Mangling by starts the full course of their glory.   5
Small time, but in that small most greatly lived
This star of England. Fortune made his sword,
By which the world's best garden he achieved,
And of it left his son imperial lord.
Henry the Sixth, in infant bands crowned King   10
Of France and England, did this King succeed;
Whose state so many had the managing
That they lost France, and made his England bleed:
Which oft our stage hath shown; and, for their sake,
In your fair minds let this acceptance take.

Exit

And Edward Duke of Bar. Of lusty earls:
Grandpré and Roussi, Fauconbridge and Foix,
Beaumont and Marle, Vaudemont and Lestrelles.
Here was a royal fellowship of death.   95
Where is the number of our English dead?

The Herald gives him another paper.

Edward the Duke of York; the Earl of Suffolk;
Sir Richard Keighley; Davy Gam, esquire;
None else of name, and of all other men
But five-and-twenty. O God, thy arm was here;   100
And not to us, but to thy arm alone,
Ascribe we all. When, without stratagem,
But in plain shock and even play of battle,
Was ever known so great and little loss
On one part and on th'other? Take it, God,   105
For it is none but thine!

EXETER   'Tis wonderful!

KING HENRY Come, go we in procession to the village,
And be it death proclaimèd through our host
To boast of this, or take that praise from God   110
Which is His only.

LLEWELLYN Is it not lawful, an't please your majesty, to tell how many is killed?

KING HENRY Yes, Captain, but with this acknowledgement,
That God fought for us.

LLEWELLYN Yes, in my conscience, He did us great good.   115

KING HENRY Do we all holy rites:
Let there be sung *Non nobis* and *Te Deum,*
The dead with charity enclosed in clay;
And then to Calais, and to England then,
Where ne'er from France arrived more happy men.   120

Exeunt.

brave

tricks

...Old Uncle Tom Cobleigh and all...

99 'no one else noble'

100-102 'God, this was your work — and we don't give any credit to ourselves for this, only to you'

103-5 'in plain open warfare, there've never been such great losses on one side, and such small ones on the other'

108-10 'tell the army that anyone who boasts about our victory, and takes praise from God, which should be his alone, will be killed'

111-12 'Can't we even say how many were killed, your majesty?'

117-18 'Let the *Non nobis,* and the *Te Deum* be sung, and the dead given a decent burial' *Non nobis* and *Te Deum* are hymns sung to thank God.

Praise the Lord!

Section Nine — The Key Scenes

Index